CAMBRIDGE
UNIVERSITY PRESS

Cambridge IGCSE™
English as a
Second Language

WORKBOOK

Peter Lucantoni & Lydia Kellas

CAMBRIDGE
UNIVERSITY PRESS

University Printing House, Cambridge CB2 8BS, United Kingdom

One Liberty Plaza, 20th Floor, New York, NY 10006, US

477 Williamstown Road, Port Melbourne, VIC 3207, Australia

314–321, 3rd Floor, Plot 3, Splendor Forum, Jasola District Centre, New Delhi – 110025, India

103 Penang Road, #05–06/07, Visioncrest Commercial, Singapore 238467

Cambridge University Press is part of the University of Cambridge.

It furthers the University's mission by disseminating knowledge in the pursuit of education, learning and research at the highest international levels of excellence.

www.cambridge.org
Information on this title: www.cambridge.org/9781009031967

© Cambridge University Press 2022

First published 2001
Second edition 2004
Third edition 2008
Fourth edition 2014
Fifth edition 2018
Sixth edition 2022

20 19 18 17 16 15 14 13 12 11 10 9 8 7 6 5 4 3 2 1

Printed in Italy by L.E.G.O. S.p.A.

A catalogue record for this publication is available from the British Library

ISBN 978-1-009-03196-7 Paperback with Digital Access (2 Years)

〉 Contents

〉Introduction

This 6th edition of the Workbook is for students who are studying the Cambridge IGCSE™ and IGCSE (9–1) English as a Second Language syllabuses (0510/0511/0991/0993) for examination from 2024. The Workbook supplements the 6th edition of the Coursebook, both of which include new material and new activities. You can use the Workbook to practise and reinforce the language and skills from the Coursebook, as well as practising additional exam-style questions. Language focus activities are a new feature of the Workbook. These are divided into Foundation, Practice and Challenge sections to support and then stretch you.

It is assumed that most of you who use this book will be studying English in order to improve your educational or employment prospects, and therefore it includes a broad range of topics and themes related to this goal. You will find passages and activities based on a wide range of stimulating cross-curricular topics and people from all over the world, which we hope you will enjoy reading and discussing.

The Workbook follows the same format as the Coursebook, with each unit focusing on a specific skill (for example, writing a formal article) within the context of the unit theme. There are word puzzles to help build your confidence with vocabulary in an engaging way, as well as grammar, reading, writing, listening and speaking practice.

We hope you enjoy using this book!

Peter Lucantoni & Lydia Kellas

> Unit 1: Sports and free time

Vocabulary focus: Sports and free time

1   Here are the definitions of **ten** words from Unit 1 in the Coursebook. Use the definitions to work out the words. The first letter of each word is given to help you.

   a   age group   g _ _ _ _ _ _ _

   b   a decision to definitely do something   p _ _ _ _ _ _

   c   encourage and motivate   i _ _ _ _ _ _

   d   experiencing in a negative way   s _ _ _ _ _ _ _

   e   a group   a _ _ _ _ _ _ _ _ _

   f   having made a definite decision   d _ _ _ _ _ _ _ _

   g   personal control   d _ _ _ _ _ _ _ _

   h   not known to you   u _ _ _ _ _ _ _ _

   i   someone you play against in sport   o _ _ _ _ _ _

   j   changes of position   m _ _ _ _ _ _ _

2   Complete sentences a–i using the words from Activity 1.

   a   For those of you who are .... with squash, it is not like tennis or badminton.

   b   The aim of the game is to hit the ball in such a way that your

       .... cannot return it.

   c   I went from playing squash for fun to becoming a force on the court after

       .... several defeats.

   d   I was .... to get better.

   e   I made a .... to myself that I would keep trying to improve.

   f   This pushed me into learning particular .... and the finer techniques of the game.

g My training has to follow a system, so it requires a great deal of

....

h In 2020, at a Professional Squash ....
regional event . . .

i I hope my success will .... the next

.... of women athletes.

> **Glossary**
>
> **strategic** (adjective): helping to achieve a plan
>
> **analytical** (adjective): examining the details of something carefully, in order to understand or explain it

3 Choose **five** of the words from Activity 1 to complete the text below.

What are MMOGs?

For those of you who are unfamiliar with the world of online games, MMOGs are games that are played via the internet or using a computer network. They can be very simple or incredibly complex. Basic online games are usually text-based, while more complicated games use amazing graphics and virtual worlds, with many players

or **(a)** .... online at the same time. That's why these more complex games are called 'massively multiplayer online games' (MMOGs).

While online gaming is an entertaining pastime and can **(b)** .... players to become better at the game itself, it also helps to develop creativity, and to support and improve creative thinking. Moreover, gaming improves communication skills – not least by encouraging people to be more aware of and to respect other

people's opinions, views and cultures. And let's not forget that physical **(c)** .... are an important part of many games, so there is also an element of keeping fit involved!

MMOGs can help players to become more **(d)** .... and **strategic** in their thinking, and to develop **analytical** skills, which are important when assessing risks. Having quick reactions and responding to changing situations are other important skills that can be improved through online gaming. Importantly, many of

these skills are transferable to real-world situations that rely on **(e)** .... , problem-solving, analytical skills and strategic thinking.

---

4 Write short definitions, or give synonyms (words with similar meanings), for these words.

a hence: ....

b regardless: ....

c feat: ....

d monetary: ....

e pastime: ....

5 Draw lines to match the phrases to make complete sentences.

Online gaming can be expensive,	regardless of her tiredness.
She was determined to carry on	was an amazing feat.
Finishing the task on time	has recently become online gaming.
While it was a beautiful picture, it	so it is not an option for everyone.
His favourite pastime	had little monetary value.

Language focus: Verbs followed by other verbs

Foundation

1 For each of the examples below, complete the verb pattern rule. Remember, verbs can be followed by the *-ing* form, an infinitive verb or an infinitive verb + noun.

A The doctor **encourages having** a healthy lifestyle.

OR The doctor **encourages his patients** to have a healthy lifestyle.

These verbs can be followed by ....

OR .:... + ...

B He **prefers drinking** fruit juice.

OR He **prefers to drink** fruit juice.

These verbs can be followed by ....

OR .... , with no difference in meaning.

C We **stopped having** a break during our matches.

OR We **stopped to have** a break during the match.

These verbs can be followed by ....

OR .... , but the meaning changes.

2 Look at the underlined verbs in the sentences. On the line, write the letter from Activity 1 to show which verb pattern each sentence follows: A, B or C.

   a Baris and Jihan <u>enjoyed</u> eating in the new restaurant. ....

   b The accident didn't <u>require</u> Altan to visit the doctor. ....

   c Mustafa <u>prefers</u> snorkelling in the sea. ....

   d Claudia always <u>encourages</u> her younger brother to read. ....

   e Diann has <u>forgotten</u> to tell his friends about the party. ....

   f Setiawan <u>considers</u> his family to be the most important part of his life. ....

   g Puspita <u>remembers</u> to video call her cousins every weekend. ....

   h Luigi and Martina <u>love</u> to play tennis early in the morning. ....

Practice

3 Which **five** of these sentences contain errors? Write them correctly below.

   a He misses to play the piano.

   b My father urged me to study harder.

   c She avoided to go to the dentist.

   d I can't imagine not to have a mobile phone.

   e We decided to go out when the rain stopped.

   f I anticipate to go to Italy next year.

   g We were required to provide two photographs for our new passports.

   h They enjoy to cook meals using only vegetables.

....

....

....

....

....

4 Complete sentences a–h with the correct forms of the verb pairs in the box.

> continue / talk   delay / give   discuss / buy   dislike / eat
> embarrass / admit   forget / visit (×2)   like / cook

a He was .... making a mistake.

b She .... dinner for lots of people.

c The teacher often .... back homework to her students.

d Nowadays, many people .... unhealthy food.

e My parents .... a second-hand car.

f I'll never .... the ancient castle.

g Don't .... the ancient castle while you're there.

h She .... even when the movie started.

Challenge

5 Write the letter of the correct meaning for each sentence in these pairs (A or B) next to the sentence.

a She forgot to pay for the milk.

She forgot paying for the milk.

A She didn't remember that she had paid for it.

B She didn't give the shop assistant any money for it.

b He doesn't remember to turn off the lights.

He doesn't remember turning off the lights.

A He forgets to turn off the lights.

B He's forgotten whether he turned off the lights.

c   I mean to do some exercise every day.   ☐

Keeping fit means doing some exercise every day.   ☐

A   I plan to do some exercise every day.

B   Keeping fit involves doing some exercise every day.

d   I regret telling you that you didn't pass the test.   ☐

I regret to tell you that you didn't pass the test.   ☐

A   I'm sorry I told you that you didn't pass the test.

B   I'm sorry to tell you that you didn't pass the test.

e   Johann tried to open the door.   ☐

Johann tried opening the door.   ☐

A   This was one option and Johann might have tried others.

B   Johann made an attempt to open the door but was not successful.

6   Write answers to the questions below, using full sentences. You will need to use either an *-ing* verb or an infinitive verb after the underlined verb.

a   What do you <u>regret</u>?

....

....

b   What have you <u>arranged</u> recently?

....

....

c   What do you <u>enjoy</u>?

....

....

d   What do you <u>hate</u>?

....

....

e What have you <u>insisted on</u>?

....

....

f What have you <u>avoided</u>?

....

....

Skills focus: Reading

1 Skim the article. Tick the best title.

The old stay young in China ☐

Keeping fit the Chinese way ☐

Chinese parks ☐

Text 1.1

[1] For a long time, China has encouraged older people to stay healthy by keeping active. Scientists at the University of Illinois have found that ancient Chinese exercises such as *tai chi* are good for older generations. Researchers say that such exercises **combine** simple movements and meditation into a series of exercises believed to have positive, relaxing effects on a person's mind, body and **spirit**. If you are unfamiliar with the idea, these exercises are **relatively** simple, but also safe. Moreover, they require no special equipment or clothing that might be expensive and limit participation.

[2] Morning exercises (or 'dances') begin as early as 5.30 a.m. and **tend to** take place in parks and open spaces near markets. This means that those taking part can buy fresh vegetables and other food when the markets open for business. The evening groups start exercises after dinner. Outdoor exercise is extremely popular throughout the day. Because of the **ease** of taking part and the low cost, there are now an **estimated** 100 million 'dancers' in China.

[3] Dancers organise themselves into rows. The front row is made up of the most experienced dancers, with the very best of them in the centre of the row. Each of the rows behind contains progressively less able dancers. All the dancers face forward, which allows them to learn from those in the rows ahead. The back row is often made up of beginners – dancers who are just learning the movements. There is a discipline about the way in which the dancers arrange themselves, with everyone determined to one day arrive at the middle of the front row and perform with the same skill as the best dancers.

[4] In many parks across China, brightly coloured, **manual** exercise machines are provided as an alternative pastime to dance. Each machine is designed to give a workout for a specific part of the body. Compared to private gyms, which can be expensive to join, China's public fitness equipment allows people to take part in physical activity that everyone can use. Furthermore, these areas generally do not have basketball courts or other outdoor sports areas aimed at the younger generation, so older people feel comfortable here.

[5] While keeping fit is important, taking part in outdoor physical activity also gives older people the opportunity to socialise safely with others in their age range and to enjoy the beauty of open spaces within cities. China is an enormous country with **stunning** natural scenery, including forests, parks, mountain ranges and lakes, but many citizens live too far away to enjoy these features regularly, so it is appealing for them to find beauty in their home city.

2   Match the words in bold in Text 1.1 with definitions a–h.
    Write the word next to the correct definition.

    a   approximate   ....

    b   attitude or mood   ....

    c   bring together   ....

    d   fairly, quite   ....

    e   usually do something   ....

    f   magnificent, beautiful   ....

    g   lack of difficulty   ....

    h   controlled by hand   ....

3   Which words or phrases are used to describe the following things in the article?

    a   equipment and clothing ....

    b   outdoor exercise ....

    c   exercise machines ....

    d   basketball courts and other outdoor sports areas ....

4   Answer these questions.

a   What has the University of Illinois research found?

....

b   What reason is given for exercises taking place near markets?

....

c   Why are there so many exercise dancers in China? Give **two** reasons.

....

....

d   Who do the dancers in the back row learn from?

....

e   Apart from dancing, what other form of outdoor exercise can people do?

....

f   What might prevent people from enjoying China's stunning natural scenery?

....

5   What facilities are there for outdoor exercise where you live? Which activities do you prefer to take part in? Is there any cost involved, such as for equipment or clothing? Write at least **five** sentences.

....

....

....

....

....

Reading, open response

Read the article about paddleboarding, then answer the questions.

Text 1.2

Paddleboarding

A few days ago, I was standing on my board, paddling against a gentle current as I made my way up a river. There were clouds overhead and it was beginning to rain, as the weather forecast that morning had predicted. The temperature was due to drop too, but the wind direction, which I'm always keen to know about in advance, was in my favour. I was trying out my new paddleboard. Until now I've always used inflatable boards; they're easier to transport and more straightforward to store. But hard boards are faster and easier to handle in a wind.

Beautiful white swans glided past me, and occasionally I saw the shape of a fish below the surface. Just in front of me, a seal raised its head out of the water, stared at me for a few seconds, then disappeared again. I couldn't believe it! In the three years I've been paddleboarding, I've never come across one in this part of the river before. Besides allowing you to get close to nature, paddleboarding is a great way to get and stay fit. It's also very effective if you need to ease stress, which is what I was particularly interested in at the time.

Paddleboarding can be done on different types of water. You can paddleboard on the sea, but you can also do it on lakes and rivers, which isn't possible in the case of surfing, for example. My initial experience

was on a canal, which had the advantages of being easily accessible to me and very calm. Although paddleboarding is fairly straightforward compared with some water sports, it's worth knowing what a good technique involves. One rule is to stand with your knees slightly bent; standing very straight, which people tend to do early on, doesn't help with your balance.

Although the technique isn't too complicated, paddling for an hour or so gives you a good physical workout. The first few times I did it, my stomach muscles were very sore afterwards. These days, I realise that my arms are much more toned than they used to be and my thighs and calves feel a lot stronger.

As with all water sports, you need to spend some money on equipment. Beginners are generally advised to buy inflatable (blow-up) boards. They're less expensive than the hard ones, and they also give you more **stability**. Also, as you're often out on the water for some time, a waterproof backpack is essential. I make sure that I'm never without my phone, just in case there's an emergency, and the bag keeps it dry. Snacks and water can be good too, but they can get a little heavy so I take cash every time I go out, just in case I need something.

Glossary

stability (noun): the quality of not being likely to change or move

CONTINUED

1   Which aspect of the weather forecast does the writer check most carefully before going paddleboarding?

.... [1]

2   What animal was the writer surprised to see in the river where she went paddleboarding recently?

.... [1]

3   What was the writer's main reason for taking up paddleboarding?

.... [1]

4   What mistake do beginner paddleboarders often make?

.... [1]

5   Name **one** thing the writer always carries in her bag when she goes paddleboarding.

.... [1]

6   What are the advantages of having inflatable boards rather than hard boards? Give **three** details.

....

....

.... [3]

[Total: 8]

> Unit 2: Digital life

Vocabulary focus: Digital life

1   Here are **12** words from Unit 2 in the Coursebook. Write each word next to its definition.

> angles (noun)   apparently (adverb)   dose (noun)
> ignored (verb)   impression (noun)   obviously (adverb)
> percentage (noun)   refer to (verb)   remote (adjective)
> supposedly (adverb)   transformed (verb)   widespread (adjective)

a   according to others   ....

b   in a way that is easy to understand or see   ....

c   not considered, overlooked   ....

d   mention, talk about   ....

e   found in many places   ....

f   a number stated in relation to a whole   ....

g   at a distance   ....

h   changed completely   ....

i   a specific, measured amount of something   ....

j   an idea or feeling you get about something   ....

k   according to what is generally believed   ....

l   physical points of view   ....

2   Complete sentences a–h using the words from Activity 1. In most cases you will need
    to use a different form of the word. Write the part or parts of speech you have used
    (e.g. adjective, adverb, noun, verb) in the space at the end of the sentence.

    Example: *It's __apparent__ that we need to upgrade the software.* adjective

a   '............................. learning' is quite a new term, even though 'distance learning'

    has been .... for many years. ....

b His condition .... after the doctor gave him three

different .... of the medicine. ....

c I can't see the picture very well. It's .... in the

wrong way. ....

d I have to .... on you the importance of rebooting

your computer after the upgrade. ....

e I'm waiting for this download to finish. It's still only on 65 ....

....

f If you continue to .... the warnings, it is .... that

the situation will get worse. ....

g There's no .... that in the instruction book. ....

h This model is .... to be much faster than my old one, but let's wait
and see.

3 Write short definitions or give synonyms (words with similar meanings) for the four words
in **bold**.

a A balanced diet and regular exercise **promote** all-round good health.

....

b I don't think the **experience** we had on holiday was very positive.

....

c He cleaned the table with a soapy **sponge**.

....

....

d My top **priority** is to find the WiFi password!

....

....

4 Draw lines to match the phrases to make complete sentences.

If you gently sponge it,	is a priority.
Being recognised everywhere you go	the grease might come off.
Providing all students with tablets and internet access	in digital entertainment.
She has a great deal of experience	to promote their online services.
Tech companies are always thinking of new ways	is part of being a celebrity.

Language focus: Adverbs

Foundation

1 Remember that adverbs are used to describe verbs, adjectives and other adverbs. They can show *how*, *where*, *when*, *why* and *how often* something happens.

Find and underline the adverbs in the following sentences. There are **two** adverbs in some sentences.

Example: *We may be <u>slightly</u> late for our meeting.*

a This app is incredibly difficult to use.

b She sometimes forgets to charge her phone.

c He didn't perform well in the test.

d The manager said he would seriously consider my suggestion.

e I spoke extensively about the challenges we currently face.

f Martine is always confident about technical issues.

g He managed to fix the problem unusually quickly.

h That's a very tall building.

2 Complete these sentences using the adverbs you underlined in Activity 1. You can use each adverb once only.

a He wants to travel .... after he finishes university.

b She .... holds the position of technical supervisor.

c He .... uses social media in his spare time.

d   Trying to finish too .... might lead to mistakes.

e   It's .... best to change your password.

f   As you .... know, our products and services are of an extremely high standard.

g   Police take identify theft ....

h   The problem was .... difficult to solve.

i   Are you hungry? Yes, ...

j   We heard an .... loud bang from the house next door.

Practice

3   Look at these sentences. Explain what the adverbs in **bold** are showing: *how, where, when, why* or *how often*.

Examples:

*We **happily** pay for subscriptions and apps.* how

***Nowadays** many people own a smartphone.* when

a   All staff members had to be present for the **early** launch of the new phone.

    ....

b   He smiled **warmly** and handed over the prize. ....

c   I will **seriously** think about the price before I make my decision. ....

d   People **usually** have at least one device connected to the internet.

    ....

e   Faizal speaks **very** softly. ....

f   Some smart speakers can play music **extremely loudly**. ....

g   That TV show is **actually really** good – I recommended it to my friends.

    ....

h   The weather app on my phone is **never** wrong. ....

4 Match a phrase in column A with a suitable ending from column B. Fill the gap in the sentence with an adverb from the box. Write the complete sentences below. The first one has been done as an example.

| absolutely | completely | definitely | immediately |
| ~~really~~ | recently | seriously | totally |

A		B
a	I . . . look forward	. . . awful!
b	She . . . recognised	advice very . . .
c	This fashion for digital entertainment	an amazing experience.
d	You should take that	different personalities.
e	The brothers have . . .	has only appeared . . .
f	That type of behaviour	is . . . unacceptable.
g	The activity weekend was . . .	the woman in the shop.
h	This new phone is	to hearing from you.

a   I <u>really</u> look forward to hearing from you.

b   ....

c   ....

d   ....

e   ....

f   ....

g   ....

h   ....

Challenge

5 Replace the words and phrases in **bold** with an adverb ending in *-ly*.
Write the word in the space at the end of each sentence.

a His teacher told him **again and again** to study harder, but he refused to listen.

....

b She wrote the answers **with many mistakes**. ....

c Matthew walked up and down **in an anxious way** as he waited for his interview.

....

d **In the end** they managed to find the address. ....

e They gave **a lot of money** to various charities. ....

f The driving instructor told him to stop the car **at once**. ....

6 Unscramble the letters to make eight adverbs ending in *-ly*. The first letter is given.
Then use each adverb in sentences of your own.

a ylefbautiul   b...........................

b mceployetl   c...........................

c foulbdytul   d...........................

d ueaenytllv   e...........................

e nfbayhisoal   f...........................

f nsgeeryoul   g...........................

g nhyguril   h...........................

h ccorrynietl   i...........................

....

....

....

....

....

....

....

....

Skills focus: Reading

1   You are going to read an article about virtual-reality (VR) headsets.
First, match the words from the text in the box with definitions a–h.

---

capable (adjective)   **considerations** (noun)   **detect** (verb)
horizontal (adjective)   **limitations** (noun)   **participate** (verb)
straps (noun)   **vertical** (adjective)

---

a   to become involved in something   ....

b   upright at an angle of 90 degrees to a flat surface   ....

c   drawbacks, restrictions   ....

d   narrow pieces of material for keeping something in place   ....

e   able to do things effectively to achieve results   ....

f   parallel to the ground or to the top or bottom of something   ....

g   things that are thought about carefully   ....

h   to discover or identify something   ....

2 Skim Text 2.1. Use the words from Activity 1 to fill gaps a–h.

Text 2.1

Virtual reality headsets

[1] If you want to travel without leaving your home, then virtual reality (VR) is an amazing technology to use. With just a headset and

software to **(a)** .... and follow movement, VR can place you in a virtual location

or let you **(b)** .... in a game or activity without even being there!

[2] VR is becoming increasingly popular, mainly because it offers an incredible user experience. However, headset technology is improving so quickly that it can be difficult to know which headset to buy. And as with most digital devices, prices can be from a few hundred to many thousands of dollars.

[3] A typical headset looks like a large, thick pair of swimming goggles and is either tethered or standalone. A tethered headset is connected to a computer or gaming station with a cable, which can be annoying. However, putting all the VR technology into the box strapped to your

face has its **(c)** .... Being connected to a separate computer can offer better-quality graphics and a more complex and interesting VR experience. These headsets have external sensors or cameras, which follow the movements of the user's head and hands.

[4] If you want more physical freedom, however, a standalone headset might be a better option. These headsets do not have the same processing power as the tethered sets, but they are still

(d) ....
of smooth, detailed graphics, and offer excellent flexibility and movement tracking. They are cheaper than tethered headsets – and are more practical. Furthermore, they give the user greater freedom to move around. Some of the cheapest standalone headsets use your smartphone as the display and processor.

[5] One of the most important

(e) .... when buying a VR headset is the field-of-view. The wider the view, the more the VR content wraps around your side vision, giving a much better viewing experience. Field-of-view is measured in three

different ways: **(f)** .... ,

(g) .... and diagonal. Some of the more expensive headsets provide 130 degrees of horizontal field-of-view, while cheaper models are lower, at 90 degrees.

[6] Another important consideration is the weight of the headset. Some can be quite heavy so it is essential to make sure that the

(h) .... are comfortable and do not force all the headset's weight onto one part of your head. While headsets have got lighter over the years, they can still weigh between 500 g and 1000 g, although there are rumours of a new VR headset that will weigh as little as 150 g!

---

3 Look at these headings. Write a number (1–6) in the box to match each one to a paragraph in the text.

a   Cable connection   ☐

b   No tickets needed!   ☐

c   Sitting comfortably   ☐

d   The experience gets better   ☐

e   Up, down and across   ☐

f   Wireless connection   ☐

4 Answer these questions.

a What **two** things do you need for a VR experience?

....

b Why is VR becoming more common?

....

c Why can it be difficult to know which headset to buy?

....

d What does a tethered headset need in order to function?

....

e Give **two** advantages of using a tethered headset.

....

f What do the cheapest VR headsets also need in order to work?

....

g What is the effect of a wider field-of-view?

....

h Why are headset straps so important?

....

5 Complete these notes using information from the text. Use 1–3 words in each gap.

a VR technology allows you to participate without ....

b Headset prices vary between several hundred to ....
of dollars.

c A tethered headset needs a .... to connect to a computer.

d Wireless headsets give more .... to move around.

e Smartphones are required for some .... headsets.

f Greater field-of-view gives a better ....

g VR headsets need comfortable .... and padding.

Reading, multiple matching

Read the article in which four young people (A–D) talk about podcasts they listen to. Then answer questions a–i.

Text 2.2

A NITIN WALJI

Jimmy Clark is a former professional footballer, and in each episode of his podcast, he chats with a guest, usually another footballer, about what it's like to play football for a living. The structure is straightforward, but the conversation often goes all over the place. I initially thought it was a bit too disorganised, to be honest, but as the series progressed, I realised that Clark has interesting things to say about what goes on behind the scenes at football clubs. Although he's a well-known person, I don't think the podcast has many **listeners**, which is odd because lots of fans would enjoy it. He was never the most skilful player, and he's aware of that. In fact, he often jokes about the mistakes he made and goals he missed, and that side of his character is appealing. He's got a very loud laugh, which I imagine might not go down well with some people, but I like him.

B STEVEN CARTER

Only a Game is a podcast that reviews video games. One thing that makes it different from most other game review podcasts is that it's presented by a young woman called Selma Ramos, and all her guests are female gamers. Selma's aim is to provide a place where young women can freely express their ideas on video games, and the conversations she has are really **informative**. Selma is clearly a talented communicator. Some people from the gaming world, however, find her annoying and make their feelings known online with silly comments like 'Why is this podcast all-female?' and 'I want to listen to experts, not amateurs'. Fortunately, Selma believes in herself and, quite rightly, is continuing to do exactly what she wants. As she has pointed out, the unusually large audience she attracts suggests that she is doing something right!

C MEI PENG

Decompose is based on a very simple idea, which is perhaps why I turn to it when I want something to chill out to. The podcaster Nick Ferns chooses a song, usually a well-known one, and asks the individual or group who wrote it to tell the story of how it was created. Perhaps because of the famous musicians who often feature,

Glossary

listeners (noun): people who listen

informative (adjective): providing a lot of useful information

historian (noun): someone who studies or writes about history

CONTINUED

the podcast has already received a lot of attention. Not all of it has been favourable; there have been complaints – for example, that some of the songs don't deserve to have so much time devoted to them. But even the positive comments tend to overlook the way that Ferns is able to get musicians to reveal a lot about themselves. At the end of certain episodes, my feelings about a song are very different from what they were at the start. If Ferns were to include new recordings of the songs by their original writers, it is likely that the podcast would attract many more listeners.

D ASHA MALIK

Untold History is an appropriate name for the podcast created by the **historian** Kathy Gordon: it covers areas of history that I've never been taught about in school. I've always found school history lessons rather dull, and this podcast has made me see the subject in a new light. Also, helpfully, it gives you links to articles, books and videos you can look at if you want to learn more about a topic. Gordon backs up her explanations with lots of factual information, which is good, but she does it rather quickly, so unless you really focus, you're likely to miss certain points and then feel lost. She also likes to include funny stories and jokes in the podcasts. To be honest, these attempts at humour tend to be rather awkward and get on my nerves sometimes. Apart from that, though, I highly recommend *Untold History*.

For each statement, write the correct letter A, B, C or D on the line.

Which person

a   says that one aspect of a podcast can be irritating? .... [1]

b   finds it surprising that a podcast is not more popular? .... [1]

c   rejects criticism of the format of a podcast? .... [1]

d   thinks a podcaster's skill is often underestimated? .... [1]

e   is impressed by how modest a podcaster is? .... [1]

f   expresses approval of a podcaster's determination? .... [1]

g   finds a podcast relaxing to listen to? .... [1]

h   appreciates additional material available with a podcast? .... [1]

i   admits to changing their mind about a podcast? .... [1]

[Total: 9]

CONTINUED

Reading, note-taking

Read the article about how playing video games can affect people, and then complete the notes.

Text 2.3

VIDEO GAMING – HOW GOOD OR BAD IS IT FOR US?

With the increasing availability of computers, smartphones and other devices, video games have become a major part of many people's lives. But what do we really know about the impact that gaming has on people?

Reports indicate that staring at moving images on a screen for long periods may lead to eyesight strain, although psychologists have also found that the ability to identify details in images, which is very helpful for some jobs, improves through regular game-playing.

Some people believe that all video games are extremely competitive and that they can negatively affect players' mood and behaviour. Such games exist, but the majority are not like that. Many are what is known as open-world, mission-based and multi-level; essentially, they are complex puzzles that take several hours to complete. Studies reveal that people playing these have better logical thinking and problem-solving skills. Both of these are extremely important in education and in work, as is rapid decision-making – something that gamers playing all kinds of video games make progress in.

Some games require players to move around quite a lot. In sports games, for example, players might have to make the movements of a tennis player, while in 'mobile games', players have to travel to real-world places in response to specific challenges. Mobile games are praised for pushing gamers out into the fresh air, reducing their risk of vitamin D **deficiency** (gamers spending too much time indoors have been assessed with low levels of that very important nutrient).

The vast majority of games, however, involve sitting on a chair in front of a screen – and doing this regularly, for hours at a time, may result in poor levels of fitness as well as specific issues such as back pain. Professional gamers are aware of this, and they often include stretching, weight-lifting and other gym work in their daily routine in an effort to keep themselves in good physical condition.

> **Glossary**
>
> **deficiency** (noun): a situation in which you do not have enough of something

CONTINUED

Most video games involve the use of a keyboard, mouse or some type of remote-control device, together with fast movements of the wrists and hands. Over time, this can lead to strain injuries in the wrists and hands. On the other hand, game-playing has been shown to lead to more efficient hand-to-eye coordination, which is of benefit in activities such as driving and even surgery.

So, there are advantages as well as disadvantages to gaming. In this respect, it is like many other leisure activities. Of course, a key motivation for taking part in a leisure activity is to achieve lower levels of stress, and that's something that many people definitely achieve through gaming – after all, it's certainly fun!

Imagine you are going to give a talk to your classmates about the effects that playing video games can have on people. Use words from the article to help you write some notes.

Make short notes under each heading.

Health problems caused by playing video games:

Example: eyesight strain

....

....

.... [3]

Useful skills developed in playing video games:

....

....

....

.... [4]

[Total: 7]

> Unit 3: Food

Vocabulary focus: Food

1   Read the sentences. Replace the **bold** words or phrases with a word from the box.

| consume | guaranteed | harmless | participants |
| actual | sprinkled | fooled | underestimate |

a   There was a large number of **people taking part** in the cooking competition.

    ....

b   The high quality of the food in that restaurant is always **certain**. ....

c   The waiter **covered** the pasta with a small amount of cheese. ....

d   Most people **miscalculate** the number of calories they eat every day.

    ....

e   Fast food seems to be **safe** but we need to **eat** far less. .... /

    ....

f   Don't be **tricked** into buying food that appears to be healthy. ....

g   The **real** number of fast food restaurants is unknown. ....

2   Choose words from the box to complete the sentences.

| outlets | considerably | majority | pressure | simply |

a   Children put enormous .... on their parents to buy certain food and drink.

b   Nowadays, there are so many food .... that it is difficult to know where to go.

c   Saying that advertising controls what we eat is .... not true.

d   The .... of customers are very careful about their food choices.

e   The prices in the new restaurant are .... lower than elsewhere.

3 Read this review of a restaurant. Choose adjectives from the box to fill each gap. In some cases, more than one adjective is possible, but try to use each adjective only once.

attractive	bright	busy	convenient
cosy	delicious	extensive	fashionable
fresh	happy	healthy	helpful	local
overpriced	polite	reasonable

Restaurant review

How many people reading this would welcome another vegetarian restaurant? If you do not eat meat then you will

probably be extremely **(a)** .... to have another vegetarian option nearby.

Next week sees the opening of Healthy Dishes. This is an **(b)** ...., **(c)** ....

place, in a **(d)** .... location, serving an **(e)** .... range of vegetarian dishes.

The restaurant can seat up to about 18 people, and the style is **(f)** .... and **(g)** ....

When I visited, the restaurant had not properly opened, but I was able to sample some **(h)** ....

dishes and **(i)** .... juices. The food is not cheap, but nor is it **(j)** ...., as all the

ingredients are **(k)** .... and 100% organic. So, in my opinion, paying slightly more for your food is

(l) ....

The young owners, Ben and Sam, who only graduated from university last year, were **(m)** ....,

friendly and very **(n)** ...., and they are working very hard to get everything ready in time for the

grand opening.

In conclusion, if you are vegetarian and want a **(o)** .... new restaurant to try, you won't be

disappointed with Healthy Dishes. I predict it will be **(p)** ...., so make sure you reserve your table.

4   Complete the table with your own phrases that express opinion and agreement
    or disagreement. Add **at least three** expressions in each column. An example
    of each has been given.

Expressing own opinion	Expressing agreement or disagreement
To my mind	Okay, but have you considered other things?

5   Write short dialogues for each of these three situations. Use the expressions you listed in
    Activity 4. Underline the expressions of opinion and circle the expressions of agreement
    or disagreement.

    Situation 1: Two friends discussing a sports event they have just watched.

    ....

    ....

    ....

    Situation 2: Two friends discussing a test they have just taken.

    ....

    ....

    ....

    Situation 3: Two friends discussing what to do at the weekend.

    ....

    ....

    ....

Language focus: Linking devices

Remember that linking devices are words or phrases used to make connections between sentences. They have several different functions, including:

- to *sequence* events or ideas in a piece of writing

- to signal a *contrast* or *comparison*

- to indicate *cause* and *effect*.

Foundation

1 Add the words and phrases in the box to the correct column of the table. Three have been done as examples.

> although   ~~as a result~~   because   but   consequently
> finally   however   ~~secondly~~   moreover   nevertheless
> on the other hand   to sum up

Sequence	Contrast/comparison	Cause/effect
secondly	although	as a result

2 Think of **two** more examples of linking devices for each column and add them to your table.

Practice

3 Choose the most suitable word or phrase from the box in Activity 1 to complete these sentences. More than one answer may be possible.

Example: *We decided not to return to the restaurant <u>because</u> the food was very overpriced.*

a The weather forecast was not good. .... we decided to risk going for a picnic.

b On the one hand, the food was great. ...., we had to wait ages to be served.

c I think I've included everything. So, ..., this outlet is really worth visiting if you're in that part of town.

d We ate delicious fish and salad. ...., the desserts were just as tasty.

e I would definitely go there again, ... only when it's not so busy.

f It was the only place open so late at night. .... we had to eat there.

4 Rewrite the sentences in Activity 3 so that they have the same meaning but use a different linking device. You may need to reorder the sentence.

Example: *We decided not to return to the restaurant <u>because</u> the food was very overpriced.*

We decided not to return to the restaurant as/since the food was very overpriced.

The food was very overpriced. As a result/Consequently, we decided not to return to the restaurant.

a ....

b ....

c ....

d ....

e ....

f ....

Challenge

5 Use any suitable linking devices you know to complete the following sentences. Use a different linking device in each sentence.

a .... to the restaurant's inconvenient location, we are also worried about the lack of parking.

b The new internet campaign will be crucial to promoting our new products;

..........................., it will help us learn more about our online customers.

c .... of the recent rise in oil prices, we can no longer offer motorists discounts.

d We have a very large order to fill this weekend. ...., we will need to bring in more staff.

e .... she ordered the vegetarian option, the waiter brought her a meat-based dish.

f We are doing extremely well this year. ...., we are not planning to expand the business at the moment.

g So those are the pros and cons. ...., we all agree to the development of a new menu for the summer season.

h The manager does not want us to stay open any later, ... the owner does not agree.

6 Write **six** sentences of your own, using a different linking device in each one.
Write **two** sentences each for sequence, contrast/comparison and cause/effect.

....

....

....

....

....

....

Skills focus: Writing

1   Use the words and phrases in the box to complete the information about how to write
    reviews. There are **two** extra words that you do not need. Do not look at the Coursebook.

> deleted   used   focus   evaluation   include   read or seen

> A review is your **(a)** .... of something you have **(b)** ...., such as a film,
> TV show, video game or book. A review could also **(c)** .... on somewhere you have been –
> for example, a festival, concert or restaurant – or even something that you have **(d)** ....,
> such as computer software or equipment.

2   What is the suggested format for writing a review? Add headings for sections 2–4.

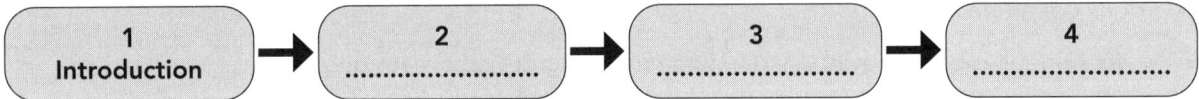

> 1
> **Introduction** → 2 .... → 3 .... → 4 ....

3   Look at this writing task and answer the questions.

> Your class recently went on a visit to a farm to see how local food is produced. Your teacher has asked
> you to write a review of the visit for the school magazine.
>
> **In your review, you should give your views
> on the visit and what you learnt.**
>
> Opposite are some comments from students
> who went on the visit.
>
> **Now write a review for the school magazine.**
>
> The comments opposite may give you some ideas,
> and you should also use some ideas of your own.
>
> **Write about 120 to 160 words.**
>
> You will receive up to 6 marks for the content of your review, and up to 9 marks for the language used.
>
> I had no idea how
> traditional the
> food production
> would be.
>
> To be honest I'd
> prefer to just go to
> a supermarket!
>
> [Total: 15]

   a   What exactly do you have to write about?

   ....

   b   Who is your audience?

   ....

4 Read this sample student answer. Which feature in the box describes each section of underlined text? Write the number of the feature in the box next to each letter. You may use some numbers more than once.

1 addition	**4** contrast	**7** information about where
2 cause/effect	**5** giving opinion	**8** question to engage the reader
3 concluding	**6** information about when	**9** sequence

Halloumi cheese – only from Cyprus

(a) ☐ <u>Did you know that halloumi cheese is now officially a Cypriot product, and can only be made in Cyprus?</u> That was the most interesting piece of information we learnt during our school visit to a (b) ☐ <u>local farm</u> (c) ☐ <u>last week</u>.

Halloumi cheese has been produced on Cypriot farms like the one we visited for hundreds of years. (d) ☐ <u>Firstly</u>, milk is collected from cows, sheep or goats, which is heated for several hours and (e) ☐ <u>then</u> cooled after it has become solid. (f) ☐ <u>Then</u> the cheese is rolled in mint, folded in half and kept in salty water. (g) ☐ <u>As a result</u> the cheese remains fresh during the long, hot summer months. Incredibly, the whole production process has remained unchanged for centuries.

(h) ☐ <u>Although</u> we already knew about the taste and texture of halloumi, we had no idea that there is a global export market of about 35 000 tonnes. The biggest consumers are Swedes, Germans and Greeks, (i) ☐ <u>as well as</u> people in the United Kingdom. This is worth nearly US$300 million every year.

(j) ☐ <u>To sum up</u>, the visit was extremely interesting, and (k) ☐ <u>I highly recommend</u> that everyone should try to find out more about locally produced food.

5 Imagine that you recently went to a food festival to sample different types of traditional foods from around the world. Make notes about the experience under the following headings.

The location of the festival:

....

....

....

The different types of food available:

....

....

....

Your experience of tasting different foods:

....

....

....

6 Use your notes to help you write a review for your school website. Your review should be about 120 to 160 words. Remember to use the four stages you identified in Activity 2.

....

....

....

....

....

....

....

....

....

....

....

EXAM-STYLE QUESTION

Writing, formal writing

You and some friends recently visited an open-air market where a wide range of street food was on sale. You have decided to write a review of the market for your school magazine.

In your review, give your views on the market and the food that is served there.

Here are some comments from friends who went with you:

> There's something special about eating outside in a crowded market.

> It's the sort of place where you can try things you've never eaten before.

Now write a review of the street market.

The comments above may give you some ideas, and you should also use some ideas of your own.

Write about 120 to 160 words.

You will receive up to 6 marks for the content of your review, and up to 9 marks for the language used.

[Total: 15]

....

....

....

....

....

....

....

....

....

....

> Unit 4: Transport

Vocabulary focus: Transport

1 Find the 15 words from the box in the wordsearch. The words may appear across, down or diagonally in the grid.

car	coach	liner	driver	bicycle	ferry
helicopter		balloon	lorry	passenger	pilot
	boat	tram	conductor	yacht	

F	A	N	B	W	U	I	M	C	O	A	C	H	W	Y	O	L	N
F	F	G	A	I	V	Q	B	C	M	W	H	D	H	Z	P	I	P
K	X	E	L	P	D	C	G	G	Y	Y	E	Q	F	D	A	N	K
P	M	W	L	H	S	O	B	V	J	W	L	Z	E	B	S	E	K
Y	K	P	O	R	Z	N	O	T	U	I	I	A	R	T	S	R	O
K	A	U	O	X	F	D	A	X	H	I	C	P	R	L	E	K	U
X	A	C	N	V	V	U	T	V	T	G	O	L	Y	O	N	A	P
C	V	G	H	R	V	C	U	D	R	Z	P	U	R	R	G	D	I
A	Q	G	H	T	V	T	L	H	A	E	T	E	E	R	E	W	L
R	F	H	S	Q	I	O	M	S	M	E	E	U	F	Y	R	P	O
O	P	N	H	W	T	R	M	B	K	R	R	R	W	B	V	W	T
B	I	C	Y	C	L	E	E	D	R	I	V	E	R	A	L	U	H

2 What or who is being described?

a It travels on water and carries people, goods and vehicles. ....

b Many people use one of these as their own personal method of transport.

   ....

c It has two wheels and usually only carries one person. ....

d This person flies planes. ....

e This is used as a form of aviation transport, but often for entertainment or leisure.

   ....

f This person checks travel tickets on transport. …………………………..

g This type of vehicle travels on water. …………………………..

h It can travel long distances by road quickly and efficiently, with many passengers.

…………………………..

3 Write sentences describing the other **seven** words from Activity 1.

………

………

………

………

………

………

………

4 Look at these **12** words from Unit 4 in the Coursebook. Write each one next to its definition.

campaigns	catastrophic	fatalities	initiatives
navigating	participant	potholed	livelihoods
slogan	swelled	strain	trauma

a causing sudden or great harm or destruction …………………………..

b describing a road that is damaged, with dents and hollows in it …………………………..

c finding the way …………………………..

d a force that puts pressure on something …………………………..

e new plans or processes to achieve something …………………………..

f deaths as a result of an accident …………………………..

g a series of activities planned to achieve an aim …………………………..

h a severe injury caused by an accident …………………………..

i   a short, easily remembered phrase, often used in advertising ....

j   someone who takes part in a particular activity ....

k   increased in size or amount ....

l   ways of earning money in order to survive ....

5   Complete the text using **seven** words from Activity 4.

Electric scooters – a guide for beginners

At first we only saw them in airports, but nowadays the number of electric scooters has **(a)** ....

and they are pretty much everywhere, providing a reliable means of transport. For anyone concerned about

traffic jams and **(b)** .... roads, an e-scooter is an excellent solution for **(c)** ....
around town.

Riding an e-scooter is no different from riding a bike. At first you may lack confidence and be afraid of something

(d) .... happening, but you will soon realise how easy and comfortable they are to ride.

In some places e-scooters are only allowed to be driven on the road, and the last thing anyone wants is more

(e) .... caused by careless riders. Make sure you get plenty of practice on a quiet street or
somewhere without other vehicles before you go into town. Consider joining one of the many government

(f) .... designed to teach you the skills required to be a safe, confident e-scooter rider.

A helmet is required by law when riding an e-scooter. Other protective gear, such as elbow and knee pads, are
optional, but if you did fall off or were involved in an accident, these pads can go a long way to preventing severe

(g) ....

Language focus: The passive voice

Foundation

1   Complete this information about the passive voice using the words in the box.

```
     main      action      agent      be      object
        past or present participle      unknown
```

The passive voice allows you to focus on the **(a)** .... or the **(b)** .... of an action, rather than on the **(c)** .... of the action. Often the agent is **(d)** .... or not important. The passive voice is constructed using the correct tense of the verb **(e)** ...., or of the verbs *have* + *be* and the **(f)** .... of the **(g)** .... verb.

2   Underline the passive verb forms in these sentences. Write what tense each one is.

Example: *Fatalities <u>are caused</u> by careless drivers.* present

a   A helmet is required by law. ....

b   He was involved in an accident, but there was no need for an ambulance.

....

c   Elbow and knee pads are designed to prevent trauma. ....

d   Government initiatives have been set up to support new e-scooter riders.

....

e   E-scooters were seen in airports before anywhere else. ....

f   Bicycles have been used for transport for many years. ....

g   Planes are flown by pilots. ....

h   Our tickets were checked by the conductor. ....

Practice

3   Identify the mistakes in the verbs in these sentences. Rewrite each sentence with the correct passive form. There may be more than one possible answer.

Examples:

In the new park, shade <u>provided</u> by many tall trees.

In the new park, shade <u>is provided</u> by many tall trees.

a   The United Arab Emirates <u>are connect</u> by a modern road system.

....

b   A unique road transport system <u>planned</u> for the new city.

....

c   It <u>is estimates</u> that people waste 100 hours annually commuting to work.

....

d   People <u>not persuaded</u> by the benefits of park and ride systems.

....

e   Parents <u>encourage</u> to allow their children to walk to school.

....

f   Recently, increased stress levels <u>has linked</u> to traffic congestion.

....

g   Since last term, students <u>are promising</u> free internet access.

....

h   The city <u>divide</u> after the canal <u>had built</u>.

....

4   Complete these sentences using the passive form of the verb in brackets.
There may be more than one possible answer.

Example: *For the holiday business, the world <u>has been changed</u> (change) by aeroplanes.*

a   So much damage .... (do) to the road that now it is full of potholes.

b   The microphone .... (not switch) on so nobody heard the announcement.

c   My car tyres .... (badly wear), so I should replace them.

d   The river .... (swell) after the heavy rains last week.

e   As so many factors .... (involve), a decision still

   .... (not make).

f   A lot of pressure .... (put) on him to pass his driving test.

g   Some participants .... (force) to repeat the exercise last week.

h   When we arrived at the airport we .... (face) with huge queues.

Challenge

5 Read about four different forms of transport. Complete each paragraph using the passive forms of the verbs in brackets in the tense indicated in *italics*.

Traghetto, Venice

The Grand Canal in Venice is 3.53 km long, but there are only three bridges over the water, so how do people cross? The famous *traghetto* ('ferry' in Italian) is the answer. These boats **(a)** .... (design *present*) to provide passengers with a quick and cheap way to get from one side of the canal to the other. Each boat **(b)** .... (row *present*) by two oarsmen, one at each end of the *traghetto*, and passengers usually stand during the short crossing.

Tangah, Pakistan

Pakistan is famous for rickshaws and taxis, but money **(c)** .... (can save *present*) by riding on a *tangah*. This is a carriage, sitting on top of two large wooden wheels. *Tangahs*, which **(d)** .... (pull *present*) by one or two horses, **(e)** .... (not design *past*) for comfort! Nowadays *tangahs* **(f)** .... (use *present*) for enjoyment and entertainment rather than as a way of covering long distances.

Bamboo train, Cambodia

If you're feeling brave, try riding a Cambodian bamboo train. These trains, which **(g)** .... (know *present*) locally as *noris*, **(h)** .... (first use *past*) in the late 20th century. Passengers sit on a platform made from bamboo, which **(i)** .... (power *present*) by an electric engine. *Noris* **(j)** .... (know *present perfect*) to travel at speeds of up to 40 kph. As the tracks **(k)** .... (not maintain *present*), the ride can be extremely bumpy and uncomfortable, but the fares are cheap and it is an amazing experience.

Monte toboggan, Madeira

Monte toboggans **(l)** .... (introduce *past*) in the 19th century as a quick method to descend from Monte to Funchal in Portugal. Today they are a popular tourist attraction, although you **(m)** .... (will accompany *future*) by two drivers. The drivers, who **(n)** .... (dress *present*) in traditional white outfits, will steer you through the narrow streets at up to 48 kph, making it a truly exciting experience.

6 Write passive sentences using the words provided. Use any appropriate tense for the underlined verbs, and make any other necessary changes.

Example: *Cyclists / not protect / danger* → *Cyclists are not protected from danger.*

a Cyclists with colourful clothes / <u>see</u> / more easily.

....

b Nowadays, the risk of head injury / <u>reduce</u> / with a helmet.

....

c Road signs / <u>introduce</u> / in the 1880s.

....

d Bikes / <u>check</u> regularly / will be safer.

....

e The world / <u>make</u> small / faster air travel.

....

f Pilots' conversations / <u>record</u> / on a 'black box'.

....

g Were you <u>stress</u> / when you flew?

....

h Since 1901, many accidents / <u>prevent</u> / strict speed limits.

....

Skills focus: Listening

1 You are going to listen to four different people talking about their experiences with a *boda-boda*. Before you listen, predict each speakers' first sentence by writing a letter A–D in the box.

Speaker 1: Well, I've been driving my *boda-boda* for 15 years now . . .   ☐

Speaker 2: I came to Uganda for work and had my first *boda-boda* experience from the airport . . .   ☐

Speaker 3: I had a couple of days in Kampala . . .   ☐

Speaker 4: I live and work in rural Uganda as a nurse . . .   ☐

A   . . . and I'm like an ambulance on two wheels.

B   . . . and it has provided me and my family with a comfortable living.

C   . . . and the hotel recommended that I should ride with Dennis because he was the best person to help me get to know the city.

D   . . . where I was taken to my hotel along with my 25-kilogram suitcase on the back of my friend's *boda-boda*.

2   Now choose each speaker's next sentence. Write the number of the speaker in the box.

a   He was brilliant and I had no idea that Kampala was such a vast and interesting place. ☐

b   I'm a properly licensed driver and we get a lot of benefits. ☐

c   We take people, especially pregnant women, from their homes to the local hospital. ☐

d   Well, he became my friend after that nail-biting experience, as I kept throwing my arms around him because I was so frightened. ☐

3   Listen to the speakers and check your answers to Activities 1 and 2.

4   Look at these questions. Write down what *type* of information each question requires you to listen for.

a   What can happen to many foreigners in Kampala?

....

b   What is recommended for safety on a *boda-boda*? Give **two** details.

....

c   Why did the speaker hold on to the driver?

....

d   Where were the mother and her baby being taken?

....

e   Why did the narrator ride with Dennis?

....

f   Where did they go on day three?

....

g   How did the narrator feel when she began working?

....

h What does she need to be careful of when driving? Name **three** things.

....

5 Listen again and write short answers to the questions in Activity 4.
There are **two** questions for each speaker.

a ....

b ....

c ....

d ....

e ....

f ....

g ....

h ....

EXAM-STYLE QUESTION

Listening, sentence completion

You will hear a student giving a presentation about a young man called Raul Oaida, who is an inventor from Romania. For each question choose the correct answer, A, B or C, and put a tick (✔) in the appropriate box.

You will hear the talk twice.

1 When Raul was young, he dreamt of becoming . . .

    A an investigator.   ☐

    B an astronaut.   ☐

    C an engineer.   ☐   **[1]**

2 After three years of research and development, Raul attached a jet engine to . . .

    A a car.   ☐

    B a plane.   ☐

    C a bicycle.   ☐   **[1]**

CONTINUED

3   At 16, Raul began . . . so that investors would finance his project.

    A   publishing academic articles   ☐

    B   contacting people on social media   ☐

    C   writing letters to managing directors   ☐   [1]

4   Raul received . . . from Steve Sammartino to launch a spaceship.

    A $1000   ☐

    B $10 000   ☐

    C $500 000   ☐   [1]

5   Although Raul was only 17, he demonstrated to Steve that he could . . .

    A   lead a large team.   ☐

    B   manage a project.   ☐

    C   deal with media attention.   ☐   [1]

6   Raul wanted to invent a full-size vehicle that . . .

    A   did not cost much to build.   ☐

    B   companies would want to produce.   ☐

    C   would not need any petrol.   ☐   [1]

7   When Raul sent his vehicle to Australia, . . .

    A   the engine cracked.   ☐

    B   some parts got lost.   ☐

    C   it came apart.   ☐   [1]

8   The safest driving speed for Raul's vehicle is . . .

    A   27 kph.   ☐

    B   28 kph.   ☐

    C   32 kph.   ☐   [1]

[Total: 8]

> Unit 5: Holidays

Vocabulary focus: Holidays

1   Find these **ten** words from Unit 5 in the Coursebook in the wordsearch.
    The words may appear across, down or diagonally in the grid.

appreciate	rolling	basically	stunning	admire
constantly	blink	breathtaking	dramatic	scenery

X	X	C	L	P	M	C	C	O	N	S	T	A	N	T	L	Y	M
P	B	J	B	L	I	N	K	G	M	T	K	Z	K	B	S	D	H
S	B	W	G	D	R	M	P	P	E	V	S	L	R	A	C	A	M
B	B	R	E	A	T	H	T	A	K	I	N	G	O	S	E	D	Y
J	W	F	M	A	E	D	Z	X	V	A	J	N	L	I	N	M	X
A	P	P	R	E	C	I	A	T	E	C	O	E	L	C	E	I	C
S	M	C	M	N	X	S	G	Q	C	G	B	E	I	A	R	R	P
G	W	A	C	R	N	G	E	F	O	G	V	H	N	L	Y	E	M
S	T	U	N	N	I	N	G	H	F	H	E	R	G	L	E	M	K
O	R	S	F	D	R	A	M	A	T	I	C	N	C	Y	V	J	N
G	F	T	Y	R	A	W	N	C	Z	T	T	A	B	Z	J	N	F
P	G	Y	Z	B	G	Q	D	I	S	A	O	K	D	F	W	O	L

2   Write the **ten** words from Activity 1 next to their definitions.

   a   to recognise how good or valuable something is   ....

   b   used to refer to the main characteristic of something   ....

   c   to quickly close and open the eyes   ....

   d   incredibly beautiful   ....

   e   to find something attractive and pleasant to look at   ....

   f   all the time, or very often   ....

g   very noticeable or full of excitement and interest   ....

h   the natural features of a landscape   ....

i   gently rising and falling   ....

j   extremely beautiful or attractive   ....

3   Use the words from Activity 1 to fill the gaps. More than one answer may be possible.

a   If you .... you may miss something.

b   All around us was the most beautiful ....

c   The higher you go, the more you can .... the .... views.

d   The hills, which you can .... from some way off, are a

   .... sight.

e   The views are changing .... because of the movement of
   the helicopter.

f   As the lesson was .... for advanced skiers, it was too difficult for me.

g   From our hotel we could see the .... hills in the distance – a very

   .... sight.

4   Write short definitions or give synonyms (words with similar meanings) for these **five** words.

a   confident   ....

b   professional   ....

c   historical   ....

d   unfortunately   ....

e   wildlife   ....

5   Draw lines to match the phrases and make complete sentences.

The travel company was extremely confident	to make sure we didn't get lost!
We booked a professional guide	the food was not very good.
We spent an amazing few days visiting many historical monuments	and we got great photos of some of the animals.
The restaurant staff were very efficient, but unfortunately	that we would be comfortable in this hotel.
There was an amazing diversity of wildlife,	in different parts of the city.

Language focus: Words ending in -ing

Foundation

1   Complete these examples, which describe the different ways that -ing forms can be used. Write the -ing forms of the words from the box in the gaps.

> frighten   write   drink   fly

A   They can be used as nouns, as the subject or object of sentences, particularly when talking about types of activity.

Example: .... *too much fizzy soda is not good for you.*

B   They can be used after a preposition, in the same way as a noun.

Example: *She sharpened her pencil before* ....

C   The -ing form is also used to create continuous verb tenses.

Example: *Tomorrow they are* .... *to Australia.*

D   Some adjectives end with -ing.

Example: *The horror movie was really* ....

2   Look at the following sentences. Which function of the -ing form does each of the underlined words show – A, B, C or D?

Example: *The hotel manager is <u>talking</u> to some other guests.* C a   The hills are a <u>stunning</u> sight. ☐

b   <u>Walking</u> along the beach at sunset is incredibly peaceful. ☐

c   We're <u>planning</u> to travel when the weather is cooler. ☐

d   After <u>enjoying</u> so much delicious food, we decided to go back to the restaurant again. ☐

e   It was a <u>thrilling</u> experience – the best ever! ☐

f   They're <u>thinking</u> about where to go and what to do. ☐

g   We really loved <u>listening</u> to all the birds in the garden during our holiday. ☐

h   Instead of <u>swimming</u> in the pool, they went down to the river. ☐

Practice

3   Complete the text using -ing forms of the words in the box.
The first one has been done as an example.

amaze	burst	crumble	eat	explore	check
offer	relax	sparkle	swim	~~think~~	visit

Discover the Isles of Scilly by air or sea

(a) <u>Thinking</u> about where to go for your next trip can be stressful! The Isles of Scilly Steamship Group provides

you with two great choices to enjoy a day trip to the islands. Whether you choose a **(b)** .... cruise
on *Scillonian III* or to fly on Skybus (the islands' own airline), and whatever time of year you are

(c) ...., you'll be sure to enjoy the **(d)** .... natural beauty of the islands.

Exotic plants, ancient monuments and **(e)** .... castles, **(f)** .... white sands and
a bright blue sea – all the treasures of the islands await you. They are located only 45 km from England's Land's

End, but they are **(g)** .... with touches of the Tropics.

The Isles are populated by a community of 2000 islanders, and there are five inhabited islands.

(h) .... just one will make your day trip memorable. Journeys between the islands are available

from St Mary's Quay, but it's always worth **(i)** .... times and tides for availability.

St Mary's, where the airport is situated, is the largest of the islands. Hugh Town, its capital, is the commercial centre,

(j) .... a great choice of shops, restaurants and cafés. After **(k)** ...., don't miss the
exhibits at the museum or a walk round the Garrison and the Elizabethan fort. There are many walks and nature trails.

> The other inhabited islands are St Martin's, Bryher, Tresco and St Agnes. On St Agnes is a 17th-century lighthouse, the second oldest in Britain, as well as a cafe for refreshments. The beaches at Porth Conger and the Cove are great for **(l)** ....

4 Which function of the *-ing* form does each of your answers in Activity 3 show – A, B, C or D? Write the letter in the box. The first one has been done as an example.

a ☐ A   g ☐

b ☐   h ☐

c ☐   i ☐

d ☐   j ☐

e ☐   k ☐

f ☐   l ☐

Challenge

5 Make complete sentences using the prompts. Each sentence should use an *-ing* form. Add punctuation if necessary.

Example: *I couldn't / hear / her / sing / because / noise*

I couldn't hear her singing because of the noise.

a see / turtle / swim by / we / start to follow it

....

b while / talk / to other people / I / learn more about turtles

....

c now / he / understand / importance of / preserve /everything in the water

....

d growth / underwater tourism / open up / Great Barrier Reef

....

e underwater tourism / put / more people / in touch with / underwater world

....

f nowadays / be / possible / explore / oceans / without / get / your feet wet

....

g   this / be / most / excite / part of the holiday

....

h   fly / helicopters / be / my dream

....

6   Write **two** sentences of your own for each of the four -*ing* categories, A, B, C and D (**eight** sentences in total). Your sentences should be on the topic of tourism.

....

....

....

....

....

....

....

....

Skills focus: Listening

1   Make a list of at least **five** 'fillers' that you read about in Unit 5 in the Coursebook.

Example: *actually*

....

....

2   Listen to a student, Aphrodite, talking to her friend Spiro about a speaking practice lesson. As you listen, tick the fillers that you hear the speakers use.

Actually	☐	Really?	☐
Hmmm	☐	To be honest	☐
I'm not sure	☐	Well	☐
Let me think	☐		

3   Listen again. Write brief notes on what advice Spiro gives to Aphrodite about each of the following.

Example: worrying doesn't help – *prepare, questions are personal, not challenging*

a   dealing with nerves

....

....

b   using your own language and phrases to show you don't understand

....

....

c   not having enough to say

....

....

d   the topic

....

....

e   pronunciation

....

....

4   Here are Aphrodite's concerns. For each one, take the role of Spiro and record your spoken responses, using the notes you made to help you.

a   We're doing a speaking practice session next week and I'm a bit worried as I don't feel that I can prepare properly for it.

b   To be honest, I'm often really nervous if I feel I'm being judged on how well I'm speaking or if I'm making mistakes.

c   But what if I'm asked something and I don't know how to reply in English? Can I say it in my own language?

d   Thanks, that's good advice. But you know, I'm really worried that I just won't have enough to say.

e What if I don't know anything about the topic they want to talk about?

f What about my pronunciation and my accent? I sound horrible! I feel I speak so differently to the people I hear on the news and on television.

5 Listen again and check your answers to Activity 4.

EXAM-STYLE QUESTION

Listening, short extracts

You will hear five short recordings. For each question, choose the correct answer, A, B or C, and put a tick (✓) in the appropriate box.

You will hear each recording twice.

You will hear a girl telling her classmates about a diving trip.

1 What did the girl learn during her diving trip at the Great Barrier Reef?

   A how dangerous her hobby can be ☐

   B how powerful a type of tourism is ☐

   C how diverse sea life is ☐ [1]

2 What recommendation does the girl give about visiting the Great Barrier Reef?

   A contact various tour providers ☐

   B study the local culture in advance ☐

   C research seasonal weather conditions ☐ [1]

You will hear a boy and his mother talking about going on a food tour.

3 Why did the mother decide to book the food tour?

   A It was good value for money. ☐

   B It had outstanding reviews. ☐

   C It visited places with famous chefs. ☐ [1]

4 Why do the boy and his mother enjoy going on food tours?

   A to try authentic dishes ☐

   B to discover less well-known places ☐

   C to learn more about cities they are familiar with ☐ [1]

You will hear a man who teaches people how to surf volcanoes.

5 Why does the man think surfing volcanoes is becoming more popular?

   A People are trying to follow the latest trend. ☐

   B People are sharing their experiences on social media. ☐

   C People are keen to experience a new type of adventure. ☐ [1]

CONTINUED

6   What advice does the man give about surfing volcanoes?

    A   increase your strength ☐

    B   use particular equipment ☐

    C   watch a certain documentary ☐ **[1]**

You will hear a tour guide giving information about visiting a wildlife park.

7   What instruction does the tour guide say everyone *must* follow in the wildlife park?

    A   pack enough refreshments ☐

    B   wear suitable clothing ☐

    C   remain in the vehicle ☐ **[1]**

8   What tip does the tour guide give about taking photos of wildlife?

    A   put your cameras on a silent setting ☐

    B   include other objects for scale ☐

    C   try to focus on an animal's eyes ☐ **[1]**

You will hear a boy telling a friend about his holiday in northern Canada.

9   What did the boy find most interesting about dog sledding?

    A   taking part in an annual competition ☐

    B   learning how to give commands to dogs ☐

    C   discovering more about the tradition ☐ **[1]**

10   During his holiday, the boy was particularly impressed by

    A   the night sky. ☐

    B   the winter landscape. ☐

    C   the unusual accommodation. ☐ **[1]**

[Total: 10]

> Unit 6: Learning and study skills

Vocabulary focus: Learning and study skills

1 Choose a word or phrase from the box to replace the **bold** words in each sentence.

absorbed	build up	engaged	equivalent to	fake	overload

a   300 million new social media users each year is **the same as** 550 new social media

   users each minute. ....

b   We are all experiencing a huge **excess** of information. ....

c   Having too much information leads to a **false** confidence in what we really know.

   ....

d   Students need to be **kept busy** while learning. ....

e   One of a teacher's roles is to help students **increase** their confidence.

f   On the course, we **learnt** all the important information. ....

2 Use the words in the box to complete the sentences.

access	discouraged	loan	reflect	regrets	struggle

a   I think he felt .... because of all the criticism he received.

b   The students needed more time to .... on their calculations.

c   Some people .... when trying to learn something new, but you
   should never give up.

d   The internet provides incredible .... to information.

e   Banks can provide a financial .... to support further studies.

f   Everyone has ...., but it's important to remain positive.

3 Fill in the gaps using **eight** words from Activities 1 and 2.

What are study skills?

Study skills are very personal and are what you need to become a more confident learner. You should have no fears

or **(a)** .... about developing and improving your study skills! As you **(b)** ....
different ways to study and learn, you will be able to meet your own learning needs in a more efficient way. Applying

study skills efficiently will also ensure you do not **(c)** .... yourself with too much knowledge.

The skills you acquire when studying English can be used to **(d)** .... other subjects as well,
although you still need an independent understanding of maths or geography, for example, or you may

(e) .... with those subjects.

Remember – practice makes perfect! You should not feel **(f)** .... if it takes time to acquire a new

skill. Once you have **(g)** .... the study skills, they
will become automatic and you will soon find yourself using them in
many different situations. Skills such as time management, critical
thinking, collaboration, note-taking and giving yourself time to

(h) ...., are all just as important in the workplace
as they are in school or college.

4 Write short definitions or give synonyms for these **five** words.

a boredom ....

b coordinate ....

c material ....

d challenged...

e ensures ....

5   Draw lines to match the phrases to make complete sentences.

The teacher gives her students	that students are performing well.
We need someone to **coordinate**	all the after-school sports.
Our group needs to collect	**challenged** usually perform better.
Students who feel	different activities to avoid **boredom**.
The headteacher regularly **ensures**	more **material** for our end-of-unit project.

Language focus: The zero and first conditionals

Foundation

1   Complete the information about conditionals using words and phrases from the box.

> before   before or after   real world   scientific facts   comma
> two parts   now   main clause   probability   possible

The zero conditional is used to make statements about the **(a)** .... It often refers to things that

are generally true, like **(b)** .... Its time reference is **(c)** .... or always, and the

situation it describes is real and **(d)** .... – for example, *Plants die if they don't have water.*

The first conditional refers to something that has a high **(e)** .... of happening – for example,

If A happens then B will/may/might/could happen.

A conditional sentence has **(f)** ....: the conditional (*if*) clause and the **(g)** ....

The conditional clause can come either **(h)** .... the main clause. When it comes

(i) .... the main clause, the two clauses are separated with a **(j)** ....

2 Draw lines to match the phrases and make complete sentences in the zero and first conditionals. There are **two** extra phrases in the second column that you do not need.

	I'll catch it.
If it rains,	we might have a picnic.
We can't go to the match	if I knew the answers.
If you mix red and blue,	if my friend picks me up.
If she misses the bus,	if we don't have tickets.
Call my mobile	if you can't find the house.
I could help him	she might be late.
If the train is running on time,	if he has forgotten his passport.
I won't need the car	the grass gets wet.
	you get the colour purple.

Practice

3 Circle the correct word from the two options in each case.

Zero conditional sentences can be written using different **(a)** *verbs / tenses*. However, **(b)** *both / some* parts of the conditional sentence refer to **(c)** *future / present* time or always. For example: *If I get lost, I ask for instructions.* (present simple + present simple) and *If I'm struggling with a problem, I try to get help.* (present continuous + present simple).

The **(d)** *infinitive / imperative* verb form, or a modal verb, can also be used – for example, *Don't disturb me if I'm studying!* (imperative + present continuous) and *If you put the towel on the cooker, it might catch fire.* (present simple + modal verb)

4   Make complete sentences by matching these phrases. Write the number (i–viii) of the
    second half of the sentence (from the box) next to the first half. Then put the verbs in
    brackets into the correct tense in the gap in each sentence.

    a   If everything .... (be) just a click away . . .

    b   In my opinion, you can't miss something . . .

    c   Success is not guaranteed . . .

    d   If they .... (do) this, . . .

    e   .... (not overload) yourself . . .

    f   If you reflect on what you have studied, . . .

    g   If I .... (fail), . . .

    h   You should challenge yourself . . .

    ---

    i   everything .... (become) clearer.

    ii   I pick myself up and try again.

    iii   if you .... (not prepare) to make an effort outside the classroom.

    iv   if you are struggling to understand.

    v   if you .... (never have) it.

    vi   if you .... (think) things are too easy.

    vii   they will have reflected on their own performance.

    viii our brain forgets or ignores much of the information it receives.

Challenge

5   Complete the following ideas with either a conditional clause or a main clause to make
    zero conditional sentences.

    Examples:

    If you make a mistake, . . .

    If you make a mistake, erase it and write the correct answer.

    I go back to something later . . .

    I go back to something later if I don't understand it the first time.

a   If you forget to bring your laptop to class ....

b   Don't bother to go to the study room ....

c   If you lose all your data ....

d   My students always perform better ....

e   Teachers encourage us ....

f   I often help Maria with her homework ....

g   Note-taking is a helpful study skill ....

h   If you follow the instructions ....

6   Write **four** sentences of your own on the following topics, using the given tense combinations.

   - a scientific fact: *If* present simple + present simple

   - a weekend plan: *If* present continuous + present simple

   - an instruction or request: imperative + *if* present continuous

   - a truth or fact: present simple + *if* present perfect

....

....

....

....

Skills focus: Reading

1   You are going to read a newspaper article called 'Why can't teenagers get up in the morning?' First, read the following information from the article and circle T or F to indicate if you think it is true (T) or false (F).

   a   During the 'terrible teens' period, all children develop a lazy streak.   **T / F**

   b   Evidence is emerging that teenagers are biologically incapable of going to bed at a sensible time.   **T / F**

   c   Despite the potentially fatal consequences of a shortage of sleep, just one in five teenagers gets the nightly nine hours recommended to keep them in tip-top condition.   **T / F**

d Although it isn't known exactly how our body clock controls our sleeping hours, it is thought that teenagers are around an hour out of sync with everyone else.   **T / F**

2 Here are eight sub-headings. Skim the article and write the sub-headings at the start of the correct paragraph.

> An easy solution   Changing cycles   Cool down and sleep
> Exams in the morning are wrong   Inaccurate body clocks   Jet-lagged teens
> Nine hours is good   Not ready for school

Text 6.1

Why can't teenagers get up in the morning?

[1] ....

They refuse to go to bed at a decent hour, complain when they have to get up for school and lie in bed for hours at weekends. During the 'terrible teens' period, most children appear to develop a lazy streak. And now it seems that being unable to get up in the morning may not be their fault, with research showing that teenage body clocks may simply be out of sync. A slight move forward in the body's natural rhythms makes teenagers annoyingly awake late at night and frustratingly **groggy** in the morning. This could have serious consequences for the teenagers themselves.

[2] ....

New Scientist magazine explains: 'Evidence is emerging that teenagers are biologically unable to go to bed at a sensible time. If teens are refugees from a different time zone, then by making them get up and go to school before their bodies are ready, we are not just making school life difficult, we are also putting them at risk. Lack of sleep **jeopardises** their future prospects, their health and even their lives.'

[3] ....

Toronto University psychologist, Professor David Brown, said: '**Adolescents**, who are usually evening types, perform very badly in the morning, which is the time of day that they are usually assessed for examinations. There are some kids whose teachers have simply never seen them at their best and that is a terrible shame.'

[4] ....

However, getting good grades could be the least of their problems, with other research showing that changes to our body clock could seriously damage our health. Tests on **hamsters** showed that changing their cycle of sleeping and wakefulness had shocking consequences.

[5] ....

His findings look bad for sleep-deprived teenagers. 'These kids are being woken in the night – before their body should wake – and are suffering something like jet lag,' he said. 'All our animal studies show how harmful this is to health.'

[6] ....

Despite the potentially fatal consequences of a shortage of sleep, very few teenagers get the nightly nine hours recommended to keep them in tip-top condition. The situation is so bad that many teenagers show symptoms more usually associated with **narcolepsy**, a serious condition in which people can **nod off** in an instant.

The number of hours spent sleeping by 9–17-year-olds according to a survey of 1000 people

[7] ....

Although it isn't known exactly how our body clock controls our sleeping hours, it is thought that teenagers are around an hour out of sync with everyone else. Our natural cycle is kept in check by two systems – one promotes wakefulness and the other sleepiness. During the day, the ever-increasing pressure to fall asleep is kept in check by hormones stimulated by light. But, at dusk, our bodies produce the hormone melatonin, which encourages sleepiness. At the same time, the body temperature cools and metabolism slows, and eventually we fall asleep.

[8] ....

In teenagers, there are two key changes. The build-up of pressure to fall asleep is much more gradual, making it easier for them to stay up later and be alert later. And their bodies start to produce the hormone melatonin around an hour later than usual. While some researchers are trying to find ways to reset the adolescent biological clock, others favour a more simple solution. Dr Ralph advised: 'Schools and universities should ideally not start before 11 a.m.'

Adapted from www.dailymail.co.uk

Glossary

groggy (adjective): unsteady and unable to think clearly

jeopardises (verb): puts at risk

adolescents (noun): teenagers

hamster (noun): a small animal without a tail, sometimes used in laboratory experiments

narcolepsy (noun): a medical condition that makes you fall asleep suddenly

nod off (verbal phrase): fall asleep

---

3 Skim the text again and check your answers to Activity 2.

4 Answer these questions about the article.

   a Give **three** examples of behaviour during the 'terrible teens' period.

....

....

....

   b What reason is given for teenagers' inability to get up in the morning?

....

   c What can sleep deprivation put at risk?

....

   d Why have some teachers never seen their students at their best?

....

   e What does Dr Ralph's research on animals show?

....

   f When and where do you think teenagers might show symptoms of narcolepsy?

....

   g According to the pie chart, how many hours are spent sleeping by the largest percentage of students?

....

   h Give **two** pieces of information about how the human sleep cycle works, and **two** pieces of information about how teenagers are different.

....

....

....

....

Reading, multiple choice

Read the article about taking notes when listening to lectures, and then answer the questions.

Text 6.2

Taking notes in lectures

Is it better to write notes by hand or type them on a laptop? Murad Awan investigates.

A few years ago, my teachers at university suddenly announced that in certain classes and lectures students could no longer use electronic devices for taking notes. Instead, we had to make handwritten notes. If the staff spotted anyone with a laptop open during a lecture, they would immediately tell them to close it. There weren't nearly as many objections from my classmates to the policy as I thought there might be, though there were some comments about how unfair it was – how hard it was to write everything that a lecturer said by hand, and how coursework would suffer.

My lecturers decided to ban laptops after reading about a study by experts in which groups of students were asked to watch a video of a lecture about 15 minutes long. Half the students were asked to take handwritten notes of the lecture and the other half took notes on a laptop. Half an hour later, all the students were given a test on its contents. Both groups of students answered questions about factual information from the lecture equally well, but those taking notes by hand were better at answering questions about ideas.

What might explain this? On a laptop, you can switch easily between word processing, checking social media, browsing the internet, etc. but the researchers made sure students were only using their laptops to take notes. They also ensured that all the students had plenty of experience of both typing and handwriting notes. One theory – which made good sense to me – was that typing speed meant students could just copy most of what they heard, but those writing by hand more slowly had to carefully select points to note, often in their own words. This involved efforts to understand the ideas they were listening to, which helped with remembering them.

But are the findings of one study enough for us to say with confidence that note-taking by hand is better than typing notes? The answer is no, and in response to this, other researchers later repeated an earlier study as closely as possible to check whether the results were reliable.

The same number of students were asked to watch the same talk and to take notes either by hand or on a laptop. However, in the original research, students were in a classroom with a screen at the front, whereas in the second study, over 50% of students watched the lecture on individual laptops out of class. Importantly, a five-year gap between the two studies meant that different students participated, which – it seems to me – may well have influenced the results. The second study also found that laptop users wrote much more than the handwritten note-takers. However, both groups in this study did equally well at answering both factual questions and those about ideas in the post-lecture test.

So, the idea that students taking lecture notes on a laptop are likely to learn less than students with handwritten notes is not supported by the latest

CONTINUED

research. When more research is carried out, certain changes should be considered. Most university lectures are quite different from recorded talks; they last much longer than 15 minutes and often include pauses for questions and discussion. Also, the gap between the end of a university lecture and when students need to show what they can remember is usually much longer than 30 minutes.

1 When his teachers introduced a new rule about the use of laptops, the writer was

   A   annoyed at how strictly it was enforced. ☐

   B   concerned about how it might affect his progress. ☐

   C   surprised by how few students complained about it. ☐ [1]

2 What is the writer's main aim in the second paragraph?

   A   to explain the reasons for carrying out the research ☐

   B   to outline the procedure followed in the research ☐

   C   to summarise the results of the research ☐ [1]

3 The writer used to think that taking notes by hand was more effective than typing them because

   A   it involved more thinking. ☐

   B   students had more practice in it. ☐

   C   there were fewer distractions to deal with. ☐ [1]

4 What does 'this' refer to in paragraph 4?

   A   a belief that more evidence was needed ☐

   B   a doubt about the methods used in some research ☐

   C   a question about how to put certain ideas into practice ☐ [1]

5 The writer suggests that the key difference between the first and second studies was

   A   the place where people took notes. ☐

   B   the subject people took notes about. ☐

   C   the identity of the people taking notes. ☐ [1]

6 What does the writer suggest for any future study of note-taking?

   A   increasing the amount of data collected ☐

   B   putting participants in a more realistic context ☐

   C   being more cautious when drawing conclusions ☐ [1]

[Total: 6]

> Unit 7: Interviews

Vocabulary focus: Interviews

1   Look at these **12** words from Unit 7 in the Coursebook. Write each word next to the correct definition a–l.

adviser (noun)	proficiency (noun)
alert (adjective)	referee (noun)
demonstrate (verb)	simply (adverb)
informative (adjective)	summary (noun)
leisure (adjective)	voluntary (adjective)
listing (verb)	willing (adjective)

a   done willingly without payment   ....

b   great skill and ability   ....

c   happy to do something   ....

d   only   ....

e   providing a lot of useful information   ....

f   quick to understand and act   ....

g   a short description giving the main points   ....

h   to show how to do something   ....

i   someone who knows you and will give their opinion of you   ....

j   someone whose job is to give advice   ....

k   describing things that are done in your free time   ....

l   writing down information   ....

2   Fill in the gaps in the sentences using **eight** of the words from Activity 1.
    In some sentences, you may need to use a different form of the word.

   a   A .... cannot be a family member.

   b   Complete the application, ... all your experience.

   c   He's an international .... to several different governments.

   d   I hate my part-time job. I .... do it for the money.

   e   Most of my friends do .... work after school and at the weekends.

   f   The job advertisement said applicants needed to be .... in at least
       three languages.

   g   The teacher .... how to use the equipment.

   h   The town does not have many .... facilities for young people.

3   Use the remaining **four** words in sentences of your own.

   ....

   ....

   ....

   ....

4   Write short definitions or give synonyms for these **five** words.

   a   insights ....

   b   latter ....

   c   handy ....

   d   remotely ....

   e   avoid ....

5 Draw lines to match the phrases to make complete sentences. Then fill in the gaps in the sentences using words from Activity 4.

These .... have really been	you can easily refer to them.
The .... is definitely	the interview is going to be done ....
Make sure you keep your notes .... so	incredibly helpful.
They phoned me to say that	going to work next week.
I don't think I can	the one that I would choose.

Language focus: Imperative verb forms

Foundation

1 Complete the information about imperative verb forms using words from the box.
Do not look at the Coursebook.

> a recommendation or suggestion   a request   a warning
> advice   an order or command

The imperative verb form has several different functions in sentences. Imperatives can be used to:

a give .... (e.g. *Come here.*)

b make .... (e.g. *Please take a seat.*)

c give .... (e.g. *Watch out!*)

d offer .... (e.g. *Check your notes.*)

e make .... (e.g. *Start with the personal details.*)

2 Write **one** more example for each of the functions a–e in Activity 1.

....

....

....

....

....

Practice

3 Look at these imperative sentences. What is the function of each one?

Example: *Don't touch that! It's boiling hot!* warning

a Shut the window please. ....

b Get out now! ....

c Make sure you take an umbrella. ....

d Don't keep doing that or I'm going to get very angry. ....

e Read the information leaflet and then plug it in. ....

4 Which of these phrases could be used to respond to each imperative sentence in Activity 3? Write the letter in the box. There are **two** extra phrases that you do not need to use.

a Don't worry, I'll drive carefully. ☐

b Why? The sun's shining. ☐

c But it's so hot in here! ☐

d Okay, I'm leaving. ☐

e No thanks, I'll stand. ☐

f Yes, that makes sense. ☐

g Alright, I'm sorry. ☐

Challenge

5 What is the function of each of these imperative sentences? Write a reply to each one.

Example: *Bring me a glass of juice, please.*

Order: Certainly. Orange or apple?

a Don't ever touch my laptop. ....

b Remember me to your parents. ....

c Take another step and you'll fall in!...

d Look at all your notes before the exam. ....

e Stand straight and look to the front. ....

f Pick up that litter. ....

6 What would you say in the following situations? Use an imperative form and say what the function is.

Example: *You are talking on your phone and your friend is shouting something at you.*

Please can you speak more quietly? (request)

a Your friend needs to see a doctor.

....

b Someone has taken your favourite seat in class.

....

c A family member wants to go shopping with you.

....

d You need to explain to someone how to use a machine.

....

e You have to tell someone to arrive on time.

....

f Your friend is leaving to go on holiday.

....

g You see someone starting to cross the road and a car is coming.

....

h You have to apologise for a mistake.

....

Skills focus: Listening and writing

1 Put the words from the box in the correct column in the table. Four have been done as examples.

~~absolutely~~	~~characters~~	common	dominant
experience	face	good	~~happy~~	incredibly
lesson	nervous	occurrence	~~petrified~~	rude
sneeze	terribly	unbelievable	unsmiling	very
worst	wrong	years

Adverbs	Adjectives	Nouns
absolutely	petrified	characters
	happy	

2 Use the words from Activity 1 to make **five** short phrases.

Examples: *absolutely petrified*; *happy characters*

....

....

....

....

....

🎧 05

3 You are going to listen to six different people talking about their experience of university interviews. Which speaker (1–6) expresses which opinion (A–G)? Write the speaker's number next to the statement. There is **one** extra opinion that you do not need to use.

A   Behaving well is very important in an interview. ☐

B   I get nervous about all types of interviews. ☐

C   It's important to be prepared before the interview. ☐

D   I feel disadvantaged in a group. ☐

E   I need to think what I am doing in an interview. ☐

F   Being prepared is one of my strong points. ☐

G   I always worry when I'm in front of a camera. ☐

4 Fill in the gaps in this information about informal writing.

> Informal writing is often an **(a)** .... to a friend or a **(b)** .... member,
>
> telling them about or **(c)** .... something that happened recently. It is important to use
>
> more **(d)** .... language than you would use when writing a **(e)** ....
>
> or **(f)** ...., for example. However, you still need to follow the basic structure of:
>
> **(g)** ....; **(h)** ....; conclusion.

5 Look at this informal writing task.

> You recently attended a talk at school about how to prepare for a job interview.
>
> **Write an email to a friend telling them about the talk.**
>
> In your email you should:
>
> • describe where the talk took place and who delivered it
>
> • say what you learnt about interview techniques
>
> • explain the questions that you and your classmates asked the speaker.
>
> **Write about 120 to 160 words.**

a   What format is your answer going to be? ....

b   Who is going to read your writing? ....

c   What do you need to include in your answer? ....

6 Read this incomplete response to the writing task. Use the clues to help you fill in the missing information in your own words. There is no limit on how many words you can write in each gap but remember that the total word count for your answer should be 120–160 words.

Clues

(a) Where? **(b)** To do what? **(c)** Use two adjectives to describe her. **(d)** What did she demonstrate? **(e)** What type of cues? **(f)** What did she maintain? **(g)** Add something positive about the way she acted. **(h)** Write a verb. **(i)** Use an additional linking device. **(j)** How much did you learn?

Hi Gregoris,

Do you remember that talk about interview techniques I told you about? I thought I'd let you know what happened.

My year was invited to **(a)** .... to **(b)** ....

The speaker was very **(c)** .... She demonstrated all

(d) .... that we'd learnt about in class and I loved watching

her use all those **(e)** .... cues. She always maintained

(f) .... with us and you could tell that she was really

(g) ....

Of course, the most popular question was about how to **(h)** .... an interview.

(i) .... was what to do if you can't answer a question you're asked. Dr Elise

gave very good responses and we definitely learnt **(j)** .... about interviews and how to do well in them.

Anyway, see you next week!

Matteo

EXAM-STYLE QUESTIONS

Listening, interview

You will hear an interview with a woman called Sophie Watson, giving advice about preparing for university interviews. For each question, choose the correct answer, A, B or C, and put a tick (✓) in the appropriate box.

You will hear the interview twice.

CONTINUED

1   What advice does Sophie give about completing university application forms?

    A   provide actual proof of your achievements   ☐

    B   highlight your relevant skills and experience   ☐

    C   express how enthusiastic you are about a subject   ☐   [1]

2   What general information does Sophie give about university interviews?

    A   the most popular courses always require them   ☐

    B   more and more courses are starting to have them   ☐

    C   certain courses want top applicants to attend them   ☐   [1]

3   What does Sophie recommend students do to prepare for university interviews?

    A   push yourself to learn new information   ☐

    B   keep reviewing what you previously learnt   ☐

    C   memorise answers to typical interview questions   ☐   [1]

4   Sophie says it is important to practise doing interviews

    A   to get valuable feedback.   ☐

    B   to see if you know particular facts.   ☐

    C   to become comfortable in stressful situations.   ☐   [1]

5   Sophie says an interviewer is trying to assess

    A   an applicant's expectations.   ☐

    B   an applicant's personality.   ☐

    C   an applicant's ideas.   ☐   [1]

6   Sophie says applicants should ask the interviewer

    A   educated questions.   ☐

    B   about the course content.   ☐

    C   how the university supports students.   ☐   [1]

7   What does Sophie advise *not* to do at the interview?

    A   take a long time to reply to questions   ☐

    B   actively lead the conversation   ☐

    C   give extensive explanations   ☐   [1]

CONTINUED

8 What does Sophie suggest doing immediately after the interview?

   A send the university a brief message ☐

   B mentally assess your performance ☐

   C write a summary of the experience ☐ [1]

[Total: 8]

Writing, informal writing

You recently worked in a café for a few days during the school holidays.

Write an email to a friend describing the experience.

In your email, you should:

- describe the café where you worked

- explain the type of work you were asked to do

- say what you learnt from the experience.

Write about 120 to 160 words.

You will receive up to 6 marks for the content of your email, and up to 9 marks for the language used.

[Total: 15]

> Unit 8: Work

Vocabulary focus: Work

1 Complete the crossword puzzle using words from Unit 8 in the Coursebook.

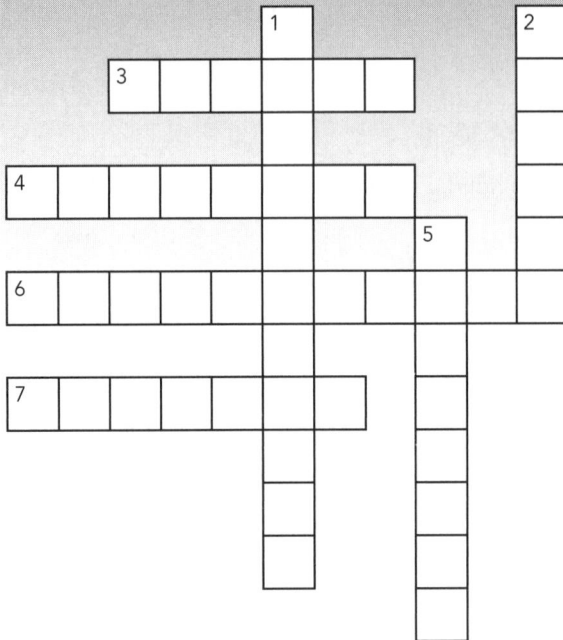

Across

3 The place that something starts or comes from (6)

4 Reaction or answer (8)

6 Important or noticeable (11)

7 An aspect of something, such as its structure, appearance or content (7)

Down

1 Changed completely in appearance or character, usually in a positive way (11)

2 A powerful effect that something, especially something new, has on a situation or person (6)

5 Officially announced or introduced (8)

2 Use the words from Activity 1 to complete these sentences. In some cases, you will need to use a different form of the word.

a Our new IT suite has some excellent ....

b You need to make a positive .... on your first day at work.

c The .... of the new company website takes place tomorrow.

d   If you do not .... quickly to challenges, you may fall behind in the workplace.

e   There has been a .... increase in traffic to the new website.

f   There are several different energy .... available for this project.

g   His behaviour this term is a real .... from last year.

3   Draw lines to match words from the three columns to make **ten** jobs you read about in Unit 8 in the Coursebook.

app		blogger
chief		developer
drone		director
food	delivery	engineer
online	listening	expert
offshore	media	instructor
social	wind farm	manager
sustainability		nutritionist
wellbeing		officer
Zumba®		operator

4   What is involved in these jobs? Choose **five** of the jobs and write a sentence to explain what each person does.

Example: *An app developer designs and produces new apps.*

....

....

....

....

....

5   Choose a word from the box to replace the words in **bold** in these sentences. In some cases, you may need to use a different form of the word.

focused   graduate   enrol   potential   literally

a   Christina **completed her first degree** in English language studies.

....

b   I'd like my research to have a main **emphasis** on language skills.

....

c   There **really** were hundreds of applications for the job. ....

d   I think there are **probably** many vacancies on the jobs website. ....

e   You have to **register** for new courses before the end of the month.

....

Language focus: Present perfect

Foundation

Remember, the present perfect form is used to refer to an action or state that occurred at an indefinite time in the past, or to an action that began in the past and continued to the present time. The present perfect is formed using *have/has* + the past participle of the verb.

1 Change the verbs in brackets into the present perfect form.

   a For hundreds of years, people .... (work) in agriculture.

   b Since the start of the 21st century there .... (be) incredible advances in technology.

   c So many things .... (change) that it is sometimes difficult to know what to do.

   d The way we communicate .... (improve) considerably in the past few years.

   e As a result of an increase in demand over the last few months, they

      .... (choose) not to reduce the number of staff.

   f Management .... (continue) to support me.

   g We .... (eat) in this restaurant many times.

   h I .... (have) at least ten messages since I woke up this morning.

2 Look at your answers to Activity 2.

   a Which sentences refer to an action or state that occurred at an indefinite time in the past?

      ....

   b Which sentences refer to an action or state that began at a point in the past and continued to the present time?

      ....

Practice

We use *for* and *since* with the present perfect to indicate time.

We use *for* with a period of time: *Martin has studied in Dubai <u>for</u> six months.*

We use *since* to talk about a specific point in time, or a time when the action started:
I haven't seen him <u>since</u> last week.
<u>Since</u> January I've been to five matches.

We use *ever* for **at any time** and *never* for **at no time** to talk about experiences:
Have you <u>ever</u> seen a snake?
I've <u>never</u> been to China.

3   Circle the best option to complete these sentences.

   a   My sister has had this car *for / since / ever / never* ten years.

   b   Have you *for / since / ever / never* seen a more beautiful sight?

   c   This laptop has *for / since / ever / never* worked.

   d   Marios hasn't visited his cousins *for / since / ever / never* July.

   e   I've *for / since / ever / never* had the chance to travel by plane.

   f   Has she *for / since / ever / never* told you what she really wants?

   g   I've learnt so much more *for / since / ever / never* the new chemistry teacher joined
       our school.

   h   He's been the manager *for / since / ever / never* many years.

4   Use *for, since, ever* or *never* to complete the sentences.

   a   Have you .... considered writing a CV?

   b   The speaker has been on stage .... 15 minutes.

   c   I've .... learnt a foreign language.

   d   He's been visiting .... last week.

   e   I've .... owned a new phone – they're so expensive.

   f   Has she .... asked for help?

   g   I haven't ridden my bike .... more than two years.

   h   He's had the same job .... 2013.

Challenge

5 Make complete sentences or questions using the words given. Use the present perfect form and add *for* or *since* if necessary.

Example: *you / ever / have / job interview?* Have you ever had a job interview?

a We / not see / Suzie / six months.

....

b Marios / never / clean / his bike.

....

c We / live / in the same town / 2008.

....

d I / be / vegetarian / four years.

....

e he / ever / visit / Spain?

....

f how long / you / have / your phone?

....

g you / ever / play / the guitar?

....

h I / never / use / the calculator / on my phone.

....

6 Write **eight** sentences about yourself and things that you have or have not done. Each sentence should include a verb in the present perfect form. Use *for*, *since*, *ever* and *never* when necessary.

....

....

....

....

....

....

....

....

Skills focus: Reading

1   You are going to read an article about a television show called *Dirty Jobs*, which was popular a few years ago. What do you think the programme was about? Tick the topics that you think are correct.

jobs that are only outside ☐

jobs that people normally do not want to do ☐

jobs where people get their clothes and bodies dirty ☐

jobs that involve cleaning things ☐

2   List **three** dirty jobs that you would not like to do and why.

....

....

....

3   Skim the text and write these headings at the start of the correct paragraphs.

- The programme's origins

- Reasons for the show's appeal

- Programme details

- Things that happen in the show

Text 8.1

Dirty Jobs

[1] ....

Dirty Jobs was a programme on the Discovery Channel, in which the host, Mike Rowe, performed difficult, strange and/or messy occupational duties alongside the typical

employees. The show started with three pilot episodes in November 2003, and continued until 12 September 2012, with a total of 169 episodes. It was filmed and shown all over the world including in Australia and Europe.

[2] ....

The appeal of the show was the juxtaposition of Mike Rowe, a well-spoken man with a sharp wit, the situations in which he was put, and the colourful personalities of the men and women who actually did that job for a living.

[3] ....

A worker would take on Rowe as an assistant during a typical day, during which he worked hard to complete every task as best he could despite difficulties, hazards or situations that were just plain disgusting. The 'dirty job' often included the cameraman and the rest of the crew getting just as filthy as Rowe. Nearly every job was more difficult than he had expected, and he often expressed admiration and respect for the workers' skills and their willingness to take on jobs that most people avoid.

[4] ....

The show was based on a local San Francisco show called *Somebody's Gotta Do It*, which Rowe had hosted. After completing a graphic piece on cows and dairy farming, Rowe was inundated with letters expressing 'shock, horror, disbelief and wonder'. Rowe then sent the tape to the Discovery Channel, which planned a series based on this concept. Mike stated that he originally wanted to honour his father, a lifetime animal farmer, by bringing fame to the less-than-glorious careers.

4   Now read the text in more detail. Use a dictionary or other resource to find words that have similar meanings to the words and phrases below.

a   presenter (paragraph 1) ....

b   jobs (1) ....

c   with (1) ....

d   test (1) ....

e   contrast (2) ....

f   humour (2) ....

g   dangers (3) ....

h   very visual (4) ....

i   flooded (4) ....

j   idea (4) ....

5 You are going to give a talk about Mike Rowe's TV show to your class. Prepare some notes to use as the basis for your talk. Make short notes about each paragraph.

Paragraph 1

- ....

- ....

Paragraph 2

- ....

- ....

- ....

Paragraph 3

- ....

- ....

- ....

Paragraph 4

- ....

- ....

EXAM-STYLE QUESTIONS

Reading, open response

Read the article about an unusual farm called Greens for Good, and then answer the questions.

Text 8.2

Greens for Good!

Located underground in the heart of the UK city of Liverpool, Greens for Good is no ordinary farm. Down in the basement of an old sugar factory, now converted into a science institute, there are rows and rows of **vertical** structures in which green vegetables are grown using a method known as hydroponics. In normal farms, crops are grown in soil, but in hydroponic agriculture it's different. They are grown in a liquid solution consisting of water mixed with minerals and other substances. The liquid is pumped to the crops along pipes.

CONTINUED

Greens for Good currently produces about 200 boxes of salad greens and herbs per day. Initially, the majority was sold to other businesses in the area, but the farm now supplies schools and local residents as well. Because their customers are all located within a 7-km radius, Greens for Good can avoid using vans or other polluting vehicles. Instead, everything is transported by bicycle.

Greens for Good produce tends to be a little more expensive than vegetables from supermarkets and shops, but feedback from customers has been positive. People often comment that the vegetables from the underground farm taste better than supermarket goods. This is partly because the vegetables have been picked very recently, so they are fresh, and, unlike on ordinary farms, they are never sprayed with chemical pesticides.

Greens for Good was established by Paul Myers and Jens Thomas in 2014 with two broad objectives in mind. The young scientists were concerned about climate change, **inefficient** traditional farming practices and other challenges facing food production worldwide. They believed that a switch to hydroponic farming in urban areas was one way to ensure food security, at least in some parts of the world. They also thought that moving some farming into towns and cities would make it easier to preserve natural environments.

Because there is no sunlight underground, farms like Greens for Good need to have lots of lamps projecting artificial light onto their plants, and they also need to manage temperature. The advantage they have is that they can adjust the conditions so that they are ideal for their crops to grow in. However, the whole system uses a large amount of electrical energy, which is a major cost – and the company's most serious challenge.

Despite this, there are ambitious ideas for future developments. The rooftops of offices and residential buildings in the city are very much part of the company's thinking. The intention is to use them to create a network of centres for growing vegetables, herbs and fruit within the wider city.

Glossary

vertical
(adjective): standing or pointing straight up

inefficient
(adjective): not working in a satisfactory way

1 Who occupies the building that is above the underground farm?

.... [1]

2 Who were the farm's first main customers?

.... [1]

CONTINUED

3   What do customers say they like about the vegetables from Greens for Good? Give **one** detail.

    ....[1]

4   Name **one** of the broad objectives that the founders of Greens for Good had.

    ....[1]

5   What is the biggest problem that Greens for Good faces?

    ....[1]

6   What are the important things used in the crop-growing system at Greens for Good? Give **three** details.

    ....

    ....

    ....[3]

[Total: 8]

Reading, note-taking

Read the article about open-plan offices, and then complete the notes.

Text 8.3
Working in an open-plan office

I was 11 years old when the company my father worked for moved to a new building. Instead of having his own small office – with his desk, chair, filing cabinets and a small window overlooking the company car park – Dad was now sharing a large, modern room with over 30 other people. He sat halfway along a row of identical workstations, and he was less than two metres away from colleagues on either side of him. He complained that he found it very noisy and because of all the activity around him he found it difficult to concentrate. Both of these issues are still common in open-plan offices today. At the time, I didn't understand why Dad was unhappy.

After all, I shared a classroom with 30 other boys and girls. Wasn't it better, I thought, to spend your day in the company of others than to be shut away on your own? Fast forward 25 years and as a qualified architect, I now design offices, including open-plan ones.

Open-plan offices first became common in the mid-20th century. Before that, each employee was usually given their own tiny room, or perhaps shared a slightly larger one with one or two colleagues. Then, in the 1950s and 60s, large organisations realised that having many employees in a single space was more cost-effective, and this remains true today.

CONTINUED

There were other arguments for the new style of arrangement. Removing walls and other barriers between people was thought to result in better communication among employees. This, in turn, would lead to improved teamwork. My father, however, claimed that, not wanting to disturb anyone, he actually took part in fewer conversations in his new office. Interestingly, some studies have revealed that my father's experience is not unusual. It appears that in certain types of organisation, communication declines in large rooms containing lots of hard-working people, who want to protect themselves against the lack of privacy characteristic of open-plan offices.

There is a benefit for employers, however: it is easier to supervise the work of a large number of people when they are all in the same room. One unfortunate consequence is that employees can feel their performance is always being assessed, which can be stressful. Having said that, many employees appreciate certain aspects of their workspaces. Large rooms often have large windows and therefore more natural light. Also, employees in open offices tend to spend more time standing up and moving around. This is beneficial in terms of health; staying seated continuously at a desk for hours on end is not good for anyone.

Imagine you are going to give a talk about open-plan offices to your classmates. Use words from the article to help you write some notes.

Make short notes under each heading.

Disadvantages of open-plan offices:

Example: too noisy

....

....

.... [3]

Advantages of open-plan offices:

....

....

....

.... [4]

[Total: 7]

> Unit 9: Communication

Vocabulary focus: Communication

1 Replace the **bold** words or phrases in sentences a–h with a word from the box.
There are **two** extra words that you do not need to use.

signalled	launched	remember	educated	focus
appropriate	yelling	community	multi-task	called

a The publication of her new book was **set in motion** online. ....

b The audience started **shouting very loudly** because the acting was so bad.

 ....

c The ability to **do various jobs at the same time** can be very useful.

 ....

d She **gestured** for them to join her at the table. ....

e Children often cannot **concentrate** for long periods of time. ....

f Our after-school club has become a very close **group**. ....

g A t-shirt and jeans are not **suitable** clothing for an interview. ....

h The scientist who came to talk to us was clearly very well-**trained**. ....

2 Use the words from the box to complete the sentences.

digital natives	tech-savvy	invented	banned	survive

a People have been .... from standing in sports stadiums for years now.

b Paper was officially .... by the Chinese thousands of years ago.

c Young people are considered to be .... because they have spent
 their whole lives using computers.

d It's difficult to .... without knowing how the internet works.

e People who are not very .... can often be at a disadvantage.

3 Complete the text below using the correct form of **four** of the words from Activities 1 and 2.

Effective communication has been part of our human identity for thousands of years, and

evidence still exists today to show us methods people **(a)** .... to help them

communicate long ago. Many ancient messaging systems use pictures, and images

still **(b)** .... that were drawn in caves around 30 000 years ago. These are

believed to represent a type of symbolic language. This later developed into pictography –

an early form of writing. Ideas were communicated through drawing an

(c) .... story, represented through a series of images organised in the order in which

they took place. These became the basis for hieroglyphics, **(d)** .... the development of

the now-famous writing style from ancient Egypt.

4 Write short definitions or give synonyms for these **six** words.

a underlying ....

b perception..

c draft ....

d evaluate...

e constructive ....

f semaphore ....

5 Draw lines to match the phrases to make complete sentences.

The trainees were given constructive	is all about perception.
There was an underlying tension in the room	you submit your final version.
Appreciating and understanding art	advice on how to improve.
I gave up trying to understand	before the committee evaluated it.
I suggest you write a draft before	semaphore, as it was too complicated.
He spent hours on the project	when the new manager entered.

Language focus: Reporting verbs

Foundation

1   Complete this information about reporting verbs using words from the box.
    There are **two** extra words that you do not need to use.

words	wh-	indirect	noun	direct object
		reporting	verb	

When we want to tell someone what another person said, we can use **(a)** .... (reported) speech

and a **(b)** .... verb, such as *tell*, *ask*, *say*, *explain*.

Some reporting verbs, such as *tell* and *say* are always followed by a **(c)** .... – for example,
Edward told me that he wanted to leave.

Reporting verbs can be followed by different patterns of **(d)** .... or clauses: **A** a *that* clause;

B a **(e)** .... clause; **C** the *too* infinitive.

---

2   Underline the reporting verb in the following sentences. For each one, write the letter of
    the pattern that it follows: A, B or C.

Example: *She <u>told</u> me where to find the answer.* B

   a   They informed us that there would be a change of policy.   ☐

   b   It was pointed out where we had gone wrong.   ☐

   c   She asked him to lend her some money.   ☐

   d   Tell him to give us that bag immediately!   ☐

   e   He maintained that he had not taken the money.   ☐

   f   She promised to buy me an ice cream.   ☐

   g   They admitted that they had spent too much money.   ☐

   h   They couldn't agree when to go on holiday.   ☐

Practice

3   Write complete sentences using the words given. Make any necessary changes to ensure
    that the sentences make sense. Underline the reporting verb in your completed sentences.

Example: *my car's tyres / tell / check / me / he / have*

He told me to have my car's tyres checked.

a   his proposal / he / me / reconsider / ask /

....

b   rewrite / advise / she / me / the essay / that I should

....

c   suggest / all / they / arrive early / that we should

....

d   with her / shopping / ask / she / go / her brother

....

e   the instructions carefully / she / read / insist / that she

....

f   some milk / buy / promise / his sister / he

....

g   point out / a mistake / she / there was / why

....

h   a new bag / ask / she / get / her mother / her

....

4   Match the phrases and write the complete sentence below.

He showed her	to meet later to finish the project.
They promised me	Mary from school later.
He didn't explain to me	to leave early to catch the train.
He taught me	it would be better not to have a pet.
Before the lesson finished, they agreed	could bring their friend.
She agreed to collect	how to find the WiFi password.
They advised us	how to get to his house.
They agreed that in a flat without a garden	where to safely keep her valuables.
They asked if they	that they would come for dinner.

Example: *He showed her where to safely keep her valuables.*

....

....

....

....

....

....

....

Challenge

5   Complete the paragraph using the verbs in the box. Be sure to include an appropriate
object, and make any other necessary changes. There are several possible answers.
The first one has been done as an example.

> ~~tell~~   tell   explain   point out   notice
> understand   repeat   announce

My friend Michael **(a)** <u>told us</u> the other day that he had a new job in the communications department of a top firm

in Athens, Greece. He **(b)** .... that the conditions were great and that he was working flexi-time

and with a team of two other people. He **(c)** .... their work stations had divisions and they were

allowed to personalise their space, but he had **(d)** .... staff rarely communicated when working.

He **(e)** .... that they were allowed to put some pictures on the wall or have a plant on their desk,

but he **(f)** .... everything had to be kept very tidy. He **(g)** .... their manager

sat nearby and watched them. Also, because he was new in the office, he had to keep asking his colleagues

how to find things. Despite that, he **(h)** .... he loved his new job and was quite excited with

his prospects.

6 Michael's friend Serene also has a new job. Read her description, then rewrite the paragraph to report what Serene said. Use appropriate and varied reporting language.

> I've got this new job in Athens, too, but it's with a small company that isn't very well known. I'm not sure if I like it yet as I have to commute every morning in the rush hour, which isn't great. One positive thing is that the people are really friendly and there's a very relaxed atmosphere. Our boss lets us do what we want as long as we reach our targets. We each have our own office space and we can even bring our pets to work if they sit quietly! Because the company I work at isn't very large, I've got to know the people and my new environment very quickly. It's my first proper job, so I'm not sure how long I'll stay, but as a first job, I'm really loving it.

....

....

....

....

....

....

....

....

....

Skills focus: Writing

1 You are going to read a report titled 'The importance of non-verbal communication'. First, use any resources available to check the meaning of the following words.

cues	exhibiting	facial	folded	genuine
	maintaining	posture	slumped	

Now choose a word from the box to complete the following phrases from the report.

a .... good eye contact

b non-verbal ....

c arms ....

d .... expressions

e sitting ....

f relaxed ....

g .... interest

h if people are ....

2 Skim the report. Fill in gaps a–h using the phrases you created in Activity 1.

The importance of non-verbal communication

[1] The purpose of this report is to describe the visit of a communications expert to our school. The visit took place last week and the whole upper school was invited.

[2] ....

There are many ways that a person can communicate with someone else. However, one thing that people are not always aware of is the importance of (a) .... Understanding these can help you to communicate more comfortably. (b) .... non-verbal cues, they are quite likely to be disinterested in what they are listening to. These cues might include:

- (c) .... in front of the body

- lack of (d) ....

- not (e) ....

- (f) ...., with eyes down.

[3] ....

If you want to interest your audience (and understand how they feel about you!), you should:

- stand with a (g) ....

- maintain good eye contact

- show (h) .... in your audience's comments and questions.

[4] In conclusion, it is safe to say that effective communication is not just about what you say. Even more important is your delivery and your reaction to your audience.

---

3 Write appropriate sub-headings for sections 2 and 3 of the report.

4 Imagine that a speaker recently visited your school to talk about internet security, but there were several problems with the visit and the speech. What solutions can you think of for the problems? Make notes about each one.

Example: *Arrived late.*

Make sure speaker knows about start time and travel arrangements.

....

a Did not engage audience.

....

b Gave no new information.

....

c Rarely made eye contact.

....

d Kept moving around on the stage.

....

e No facial expressions.

....

5 Your teacher has asked you to write a report about the speaker's visit. Say what the problems were and suggest how the speaker could improve if he returns next year.

Here are some comments from students in your class:

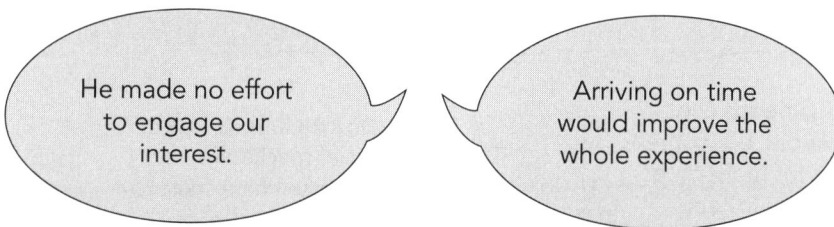

He made no effort to engage our interest.

Arriving on time would improve the whole experience.

Now write the report for your teacher.

The comments above may give you some ideas, and you should also use some ideas of your own.

Write about 120 to 160 words.

....

....

....

....

....

....

....

....

....

....

....

....

EXAM-STYLE QUESTION

Writing, formal writing

Your class has been looking at the role that social media plays in the lives of teenagers today, and you have carried out a survey among students in your school. Your teacher has asked you to write a report in which you explain what you found out in your survey.

In your report, you should explain what the students use social media for, what they think are the benefits of using it and whether they think it has any negative aspects.

Here are some comments from students in your class:

All my friends use social media, but some spend a lot more time on it than others.

The conversations I have on social media are very different from face-to-face conversations I have.

Now write a report for your teacher.

The comments above may give you some ideas, and you should also use some ideas of your own.

Write about 120 to 160 words.

You will receive up to 6 marks for the content of your report, and up to 9 marks for the language used.

[Total: 15]

CONTINUED

> Unit 10: Education

Vocabulary focus: Education

1 Look at this list of **15** verbs. Choose suffixes from the box to turn the verbs into nouns, making any spelling changes that are necessary.

-tion	-ment	-ure	-iasm	-sion	-ledge	-ence

achieve ....   educate ....   include ....

correct ....   enthuse ....   involve ....

differ ....   establish ....   know ....

disappoint ....   excite ....   participate ....

discuss ....   govern ....   please ....

2 Match the correct definitions to **eight** verbs from Activity 1.

a to be unlike something or someone else, either physically or in another way

....

b to be or become involved in an activity ....

c to make someone have strong feelings of happiness and enthusiasm ....

d to control and direct the public business of a country, city, group of people, etc.

....

e to express excitement or great interest in something ....

f to fail to satisfy someone or their hopes, or to make someone feel unhappy

....

g to include someone in something ....

h to succeed in finishing something or reaching an aim, especially after a lot of work

or effort ....

3 Use the noun form of the other **seven** words to complete these sentences.

   a He has a very limited .... of Italian.

   b This part is wrong, so you need to make a .... here.

   c It is important for every child to receive a good ....

   d It was a real .... meeting all your friends.

   e She was considered for .... in the first team.

   f The .... of new traffic laws is our priority now.

   g The subject is still under .... and we'll let you know our decision later.

4 Choose words from columns A and B to make noun + noun or adjective + noun combinations. Write the combinations in column C.

A	B	C
air	age	
desert	camping	
international	card	
digital	club	
topic	conditioning	
literacy	qualifications	
education	rankings	
comprehension	reading	
book	skills	
electronic	tests	

5 Choose **five** of your answers from Activity 4 and use them in sentences of your own.

   ....

   ....

   ....

   ....

   ....

Language focus: More conditionals

Foundation

1   Look at these conditional sentences. In the boxes, write whether each sentence is zero (0), first (1), second (2) or third (3) conditional.

Example: *If I study hard this afternoon, I'll go to the cinema later.* `1`

   a   If I were you, I wouldn't watch that movie. ☐

   b   If you are trying to mix oil and water, it is impossible. ☐

   c   She would have passed the test if she had studied harder. ☐

   d   She could miss the train if she doesn't leave now. ☐

   e   Water boils if you heat it to 100 degrees Celsius. ☐

   f   If you have taken your medicine, you'll get better quickly. ☐

   g   You might have got very wet if you hadn't taken your umbrella. ☐

   h   If I had his number, I could call him. ☐

2   For each sentence (a–h) in Activity 1, write the verb tense used.

Example: *If I study hard this afternoon, I'll go to the cinema later.*

present simple (study) + modal future (will go)

   a   ....

   b   ....

   c   ....

   d   ....

   e   ....

   f   ....

   g   ....

   h   ....

Practice

3 Draw lines to match the phrases to make complete conditional sentences.

If I had tried harder,	I would have cooked dinner for you.
If you freeze water	if they don't get enough water.
Plants die	if you make a mistake.
If we get separated,	if you'd told me about the trip.
Nobody will notice	it becomes a solid.
If you drop that glass,	it might break.
If you went to bed earlier,	I might have won the race.
If I could play better,	meet me outside the supermarket.
If I'd known you were coming,	they'd pick me for the team.
I could have joined you	you wouldn't feel so tired.

4 Use your own ideas to complete these conditional sentences.

Example: *If a baby is hungry, it cries.*

a   If I'd known you were in hospital, ...

b   ...., she would have gone.

c   If it snows, ...

d   If you don't hurry, ...

e   ...., you will hurt yourself.

f   .... if the weather is good.

Challenge

5 Put the verbs in brackets in the correct tenses to make conditional sentences.

Example: *If I <u>were</u> (be) president, I <u>would change</u> (change) many things.*

a My sister .... (cry) if she .... (watch) this movie.

b You .... (understand) the joke if you .... (speak) German.

c I .... (eat) this if it .... (taste) better.

d If I .... (know) you were listening, I .... (not make) that comment.

e If we .... (see) the news about the accident, we

.... (not go) by car.

6 Look at the following information and situations. Write a conditional sentence for each one.

Example: *Joshua failed his driving test.*

If Joshua had practised more, he might have passed his driving test.

a I was too late to enter the stadium for the match.

....

b I've decided to ignore the weather forecast today.

....

c You should give your pets plenty of water.

....

d I'm going to add the sugar before the milk.

....

e I woke up late and missed the sunrise.

....

f I don't have enough money to buy these trainers.

....

Skills focus: Speaking

1   You are going to listen to someone talking about a girl called Bimla, who always wanted to go to university. Before you listen, write the **eight** words in the box next to the correct definition a–h.

> constructive (adjective)   nonetheless (adverb)
> sacrifices (noun)   academic (adjective)   contribute (verb)
> graduate (noun)   reputation (noun)   atmosphere (noun)

a   a person who has a degree from a university or college ....

b   despite what has just been said or done ....

c   things that are valuable to you that you give up in order to help someone else

....

d   describing things that are intended to help someone or improve understanding

....

e   relating to schools, especially colleges and universities ....

f   the character, feeling or mood of a place or situation ....

g   the general opinion that people have about someone or something ....

h   to help by providing money or support ....

2   Use the eight words from Activity 1 to complete these **eight** phrases that you will hear in the talk.

a   But they accepted the idea when they thought about the advantages of having

a university .... in the family.

b   Although her teachers had always told her that she would do well at university, she

.... believed that other students would be better than her.

c   She found that she could use the time sitting on the train in a .... way.

d   That wasn't a priority for her because she knew that she wasn't the only one making

.... for her studies.

e She'd always understood that her parents would depend on the children to

.... money to the home.

f The .... was usually peaceful.

g The university had a good .... and she thought she wouldn't get in.

3 Listen to the information about Bimla. For each question, circle the letter of the correct answer, A, B or C.

a Bimla was worried about

  A going to university.

  B her exam results.

  C other students.

b Some of Bimla's friends said that

  A she shouldn't go to university.

  B her exam results were not good enough.

  C university was for everyone.

c Bimla's parents

  A did not ask her to help by giving them money.

  B did not want her to go to university at first.

  C did not understand the advantages of going to university.

d According to the speaker, Bimla studied medicine

  A at home.

  B on the train.

  C at work.

e How does Bimla feel now about her university experience?

  A positive

  B negative

  C frightened

4   Arrange to meet one of your classmates online, at school or somewhere else. Together, think about the topic of education as preparation for work, and then audio or video record a conversation about it. Try to use language and ideas from this unit, as well as your own ideas. Your conversation should last no more than two minutes.

EXAM-STYLE QUESTION

Speaking, interview

Look at the card, which contains questions on the topic of education.

In pairs, first decide who will play the interviewer and who will play the student. Then role-play the interview. The student playing the interviewer should ask the questions in the box. (If you are doing this at home, try recording your answers to the questions instead.) Your interview should last 2–3 minutes.

When you finish, change roles and role-play the interview again.

Education

- What is your typical school day like?

- Can you tell me about a time when you had to work very hard at school, and what you did?

- Do you think learning with a teacher is better than learning on your own?

Vocabulary focus: Human achievements

1 Match definitions a–i with the words from the box. Write the words next to the definition. Then write them in the table to find the name of someone from Unit 11 in the Coursebook. The first one has been done as an example.

| obstacle | hypothermia | synchronised | ~~commitment~~ |
| disqualification | misleading | dehydration | role-model | inhabited |

a   a promise or firm decision to do something   commitment

b   describing something that is believable but not true   ....

c   a condition in which the body is extremely cold   ....

d   lived in   ....

e   the removal of someone from a competition   ....

f   something that gets in your way   ....

g   a condition when the body does not have enough water   ....

h   someone admirable who others can look up to and copy   ....

i   describing things happening at the same time   ....

a					C	O	M	M	I	T	M	E	N	T				
b																		
c																		
d																		
e																		
f																		
g																		
h																		
i																		

2 Write the definitions from the box next to the correct word a–e.

> given a job   honours/prizes   located
> project   university qualification

a venture ....

b based ....

c recruited...

d degree..

e awards...

3 Complete this text about the person whose name you discovered in Activity 1.
Write the person's name in gap a, then use the words from Activity 2 to fill in b–f.

> **(a)** .... is an Egyptian businesswoman who completed a **(b)** .... in civil
>
> engineering. She was **(c)** .... by a construction company **(d)** .... in Dubai.
>
> She has received many **(e)** ...., but specifically for her **(f)** .... to build
> low-cost homes for first-time buyers.

4 Are the following definitions true (T) or false (F)? Write the letter on the line.
Include the correct definition for any that are false.

a peninsula: a long lake that flows into the sea

....

b volunteer: a person who helps others for no payment

....

c precursor: something that happened previously that affects the present

....

d debut: to present something for the last time

....

e capsize: to overturn in water

....

f   founder: someone who manages an organisation

....

5   Use the words from Activity 4 to complete the following sentences.

a   Her acting .... met with great success.

b   The storm caused the boat to ...., throwing everyone
     on board into the sea.

c   The .... of that technology company is one of the world's
     wealthiest people.

d   Many rare birds live on the .... because it is difficult for people
     to access.

e   Scientists were afraid that the development of the land would be the

     .... to the destruction of important habitats.

f   As a ...., he looked after many different animals.

Language focus: Past perfect simple and past perfect continuous

Foundation

1   Use the words in the box to complete the information about the past perfect form.
     Do not look at the information in the Coursebook.

both	certain point	completed	events	going on
continuous	past	point	took place	two	simple

There are **(a)** .... forms of the past perfect: simple and continuous. They are

(b) .... used to describe **(c)** .... that took place up to a certain

(d) .... in the **(e)** ....

The past perfect **(f)** .... describes a **(g)** .... action or event.
It is formed with *had* + the past participle of the verb.

The past perfect **(h)** .... describes an action or event that was still **(i)** .... up to

a **(j)** .... in the past, before something else **(k)** .... It is formed by *had been* +

-ing form of the verb. The past perfect continuous is usually followed by *when* or *before* + past simple.

2 Underline the past perfect verbs in these sentences. Say if they are past perfect simple (PPS) or past perfect continuous (PPC).

Example: *They had been to the same restaurants many times.* PPS

a The room was really dirty as they hadn't cleaned it for weeks. ....

b At last the taxi came. I had been waiting ages. ....

c By the time we arrived at the cinema last night, the movie had already begun.

....

d My dad had been working as a police officer for five years before he was promoted.

....

e We were best friends. We had known each other for ages. ....

f Our neighbours were very apologetic that they had been making so much noise.

....

Practice

3 Put the verbs in brackets into the past perfect simple form.

Example: *My phone didn't work because I had forgotten the charger.* forget

a When she went out to the cinema, she .... her homework. (already/do)

b He .... to the countryside before last year. (not/be)

c If you .... to me, you would have got that job. (listen)

d My brother .... home by the time I arrived. (leave)

e She got upset when she realised she .... her laptop. (lose)

f The children were really hungry because they .... for ages. (not eat)

4 Choose verbs from the box and use them in the past perfect continuous form to complete sentences a–f.

> | knock | drink | operate | practise | wait | run |

a He .... milk out of the carton when his dad walked into the kitchen.

b Te Dang .... up the hill at the time she fell and broke her leg.

c The old computers .... well since 2001.

d Manuel .... at the door for more than five minutes before Jeff finally heard him.

e They .... for over an hour when it started to rain.

f How long (they) .... before the bus arrived?

Challenge

5 Complete the sentences using either the present perfect simple or present perfect continuous form of the verbs in brackets.

a This was the first time we .... (eat) at the restaurant although we

   .... (visit) the area for many years.

b She bought her first car when she was 28. She .... (save) money for many years.

c He .... (worry) for a long time about his choice of subjects, and by

   the end of the second term he .... (decide) to change his course.

d Even though she believed her job was safe, she .... (call) several other companies to see if they had any vacancies.

e We .... (apply) in advance for tickets, but we had no luck.

f On the way to Italy we .... (fly) in a brand new aeroplane. However, on the way back the plane was very old.

6 Look at the following text about the famous explorer Captain Robert Scott. Write the verbs in brackets in the gaps using either the past simple or the past perfect simple.

Robert Scott: The return journey

By January 1912, only five men remained: Scott, Wilson, Oates,

Bowers and Evans. On 17 January, they **(a)** .... (reach) the pole, only to find that a Norwegian party, led by Roald

Amundsen, **(b)** .... (beat) them to it. Inside a small tent supported by a single bamboo stick flying a Norwegian flag was a record of the five explorers who

(c) .... (be) the first to reach the South Pole.

Deeply disappointed, Scott and his team **(d)** ....

(start) the 1500 km journey back to base. Sadly, the return was unsuccessful. It was not until 12 November that a search party

(e) .... (find) Scott's tent which **(f)** .... (bury) in snow.

Skills focus: Reading

1 Look at these four names. Have you heard of any of these people? Do you know what they have achieved? Match the names with each person's area of interest and achievements. Write the letter in the box.

a   Jaden Ashman ☐

b   Malala Yousafzai ☐

c   Cory Nieves ☐

d   Uğur Şahin ☐

A   campaigner for girls' education, specifically in Asia

B   owner of one of America's most famous cookie companies

C   winner of the Fortnite World Cup

F   head of the team of scientists behind the Pfizer COVID-19 vaccine

2 Check your answers to Activity 1 by skimming the text and underlining the words that helped you find the correct answer.

Text 11.1

Famous names

Certain people's names have become linked with particular events in life, and will always be recognisable. The names below are from all different eras, ages and backgrounds, and their achievements vary just as much.

Cory Nieves, also known as 'Mr Cory', became the owner of Mr Cory's Cookies (biscuits) at the age of six! He had a lot of ambition and started out by selling hot cocoa to raise money. His determination and hard work eventually earned him the financial support he needed to attend college, but he continued to research how best to meet his customers' needs. His success and award-winning cookie recipes have established his position among America's leading companies and brands.

Malala Yousafzai was born in July 1997. She is a Pakistani blogger and children's rights activist who is committed to maintaining the right of education for girls. In October 2012, she was shot on her way home from school by people who opposed her ideas. Yousafzai's achievements include being awarded the Nobel Peace Prize in 2014, being voted one of the most **influential** people in the world, and speaking at the United Nations headquarters about access to education for all.

Uğur Şahin is a Turkish-born German who initially carried out research in the field of oncology – the branch of medicine that deals in the treatment of cancer. More recently, however, he has become famous for helping to develop one of the world's major vaccines against COVID-19. Şahin's family was originally from Turkey, but they moved to Germany when he was four years old and he later studied medicine there. As a result of his team's success in their development of major vaccines, he has become one of Germany's wealthiest people.

Jaden Ashman is the youngest electronic sports millionaire in terms of earnings from a single tournament. Jaden started his gaming career around the age of 15 by playing all types of video games, spending almost 100% of his time improving his skills Initially his parents had concerns that he was spending too much time on his computer, and they were worried that his schoolwork would suffer. But when he was invited to the Fortnite World Cup, they realised that their son had a real talent!

3 For each of the following questions, choose one of the four people in Text 11.1. Write their name on the line.

Which person

> **Glossary**
>
> **influential** (adjective): having a lot of influence on people

a started life as an immigrant? ....

b continued their work after a personal tragedy? ....

c was a young entrepreneur with humble beginnings? ....

d loves playing games for a living? ....

e sold drinks to make money? ....

f   wants to improve education for everyone? ....

g   caused their parents concern about their education? ....

h   has been involved in medicine for most of their life? ....

EXAM-STYLE QUESTION

Reading, multiple matching

Read the article about four people with very unusual abilities. Then answer questions a–i.

Text 11.2

A JO CAMERON

During her life, retired teacher Jo Cameron has experienced broken limbs, cuts, burns, childbirth and surgery – all with hardly any need for pain relief. But for many years, she never realised that this was unusual. At the age of 65, she had two operations that are normally very painful – but Jo felt almost nothing. Puzzled doctors discovered that Jo has very rare **genetic** differences, which **suppress** pain and anxiety and increase happiness. It turned out that Jo's son has the same condition and that her late father had almost certainly had it too. Since then, Jo has allowed scientists to study her closely in the hope that they will make discoveries about how pain works, which could be very important in treating illnesses. When this research was reported in the media, 80 people worldwide came forward claiming to have the same condition as Jo. Having been uneasy at the thought that her family might be unique, this brought Jo some comfort.

B SCOTT FLANSBURG

'Human calculator' Scott Flansburg can mentally add, subtract, multiply, divide, and find square and cube roots almost instantly, with perfect accuracy. As a nine-year-old, he created methods for solving maths problems that were very different from the standard approaches being taught in his school. Despite his extraordinary talent, Flansburg never went on to study maths at university, but he has found ways of putting his ability to good use. For a while, finance companies employed him to analyse international trading figures, but increasingly sophisticated software meant his skills could be replaced. Nowadays, he mainly gives talks in schools and universities. His aim is to help people understand that numbers can be beautiful and exciting to work with. He says that many people have a hidden talent for maths – and he wants to help them find it!

Glossary

genetic (adjective): belonging or related to genes (parts of the DNA in cells)

suppress (verb): to end something by force

C DEREK PARAVICINI

Derek Paravicini has been blind since his birth in 1979, but playing the piano is as easy for him as breathing. Whenever he hears a piece of music, he can instantly copy it on the piano, and it stays in his memory. At the same time, Derek doesn't read or write and needs help with many simple tasks that others find easy. When he was 18 months old, Derek was given a toy piano and was immediately able to play it. At four, his parents arranged lessons for him. For a while, Derek refused to do what the teacher asked him to do. The teacher continued working with him, however, and by the age of eight Derek's piano-playing was so good that he was invited to perform on television shows. Since then, Derek has made records and performed live for audiences all over the world.

D REBECCA SHARROCK

Rebecca Sharrock has a condition called Highly Superior Autobiographical Memory (HSAM): she remembers every minute of her life. In fact, her brain just isn't able to forget. This might sound great, but included in her memories are all the anxieties, embarrassments and disappointments she has ever experienced. Scientists estimate that just 60 people in the world have this condition and they are keen to investigate how Rebecca's extraordinary mind and memory work. Using a range of tests, they hope to make discoveries that will lead to improved treatments for people who suffer from brain damage and extreme memory loss. Knowing she could make a valuable contribution to science, Rebecca can see the good side of her condition in a way she wasn't able to in the past.

For each statement, write the correct letter A, B, C or D on the line.

Which person

a   has more positive feelings about their unusual ability than in the past?   .... [1]

b   has been in the public eye since childhood?   .... [1]

c   was relieved to learn that there are others with a similar ability?   .... [1]

d   was unwilling to follow instructions when younger?   .... [1]

e   has been affected by developments in technology?   .... [1]

f   struggles to deal with one effect of their unusual ability?   .... [1]

g   is unable to carry out many everyday activities on their own?   .... [1]

h   probably inherited their unusual ability?   .... [1]

i   uses their unusual ability to inspire others?   .... [1]

[Total: 9]

> Unit 12: Organisations and volunteers

Vocabulary focus: Organisations and volunteers

1 Find the **eight** words from the box in the wordsearch. The words may appear across, down or diagonally in the grid.

agriculture	boost	caring	craft	currently	outreach
	throughout		unique		

B	G	C	T	G	Q	J	G	T	G	O	Q	A	C	C	Q	X	E
T	A	Z	L	N	J	L	D	M	J	U	L	G	O	U	F	W	N
E	H	S	J	D	Y	O	I	G	T	T	B	R	N	R	Z	A	U
T	B	R	E	C	G	D	A	B	R	R	C	I	F	R	K	I	R
V	R	V	O	D	N	Z	T	O	A	E	L	C	I	E	W	R	S
I	F	K	Q	U	P	P	T	O	N	A	R	U	D	N	L	Z	E
O	N	Q	O	V	G	U	C	S	G	C	B	L	E	T	V	K	R
B	X	T	B	M	Q	H	T	T	E	H	T	T	N	L	R	C	I
T	N	D	H	V	A	P	O	I	Y	F	I	U	C	Y	C	A	E
D	Q	Y	B	M	P	A	N	U	G	H	X	R	E	M	N	D	S
Q	R	U	N	I	Q	U	E	X	T	C	A	E	R	Y	G	M	W
I	C	R	A	F	T	C	A	R	I	N	G	N	N	N	L	H	E

2 Now find **four** more words from Unit 12 in the Coursebook in the grid.

3 Write **eight** of the words from the grid next to the correct definitions. One has been done as an example.

a protecting or looking after something or someone   *caring*

b a set of things of similar type   ....

c certainty about your ability to do something   ....

d   to improve or increase something   ....

e   to be focused on or in a particular place   ....

f   an activity in which something is made by hand   ....

g   the only one of its kind   ....

h   during the whole time   ....

4   Circle the correct word from each pair to complete the sentences.

Example: *The weekend trips focus on the* (observation) */ foundation of nature and wildlife.*

a   Exploring nature gives children *invaluable / accumulated* knowledge.

b   Many people are very *trained / concerned* about damage to the environment.

c   The group hopes to *create / broaden* young people's understanding of global issues.

d   Human-made disasters are *appealing / threatening* our way of life.

e   The amount of single-use plastic has decreased *dramatically / potentially* in recent years.

5   Use the other word in each pair to write **five** more sentences of your own.

Example: *After-school clubs provide a* <u>foundation</u> *for different types of learning.*

....

....

....

....

....

Language focus: Non-defining relative clauses

Foundation

1   Circle the correct word from each pair to complete the paragraph about non-defining relative clauses.

> There are two types of relative clauses: defining and non-defining.
>
> A defining relative clause defines the *subject / object* of the sentence, so we understand who or what it is talking about. It is *necessary / not necessary* to the sense of the sentence.

A non-defining relative clause gives *essential / additional* detail or information about the subject of the sentence. However, if you remove the non-defining clause, the sentence will *still / not* make sense. For example:

I'm looking for the person whose car is blocking mine. (defining)

I'm looking for the person from that house there, whose car is blocking mine. (non-defining)

A relative pronoun / an object pronoun or an adverb is always used to start a non-defining relative clause, and it is always separated from the rest of the sentence by *full stops / commas*.

2   Draw a line through the clauses that can be omitted from the following sentences.

Example: *We talked about our holiday, ~~which is arranged for next month~~.*

a   They had to feed the poor cat, which stole the little boy's dinner.

b   Have you been back to the restaurant that we went to last year?

c   There's Christina, who works in the factory up the road, coming out of the bakery.

d   To get to Alberto's house, take the second road on the left, which has lots of tall trees along it.

e   The lady who lives next door has offered to look after my house while I'm away.

f   Nektarios, who offered to lend me some money, is a great friend.

g   My grandmother, who's nearly 90, swims every day.

h   He received very bad grades for his exams, which he hardly studied for.

Practice

3   Some of the following sentences have mistakes in them. Write the sentences correctly on the lines. Put a tick (✓) on the line for any that do not contain mistakes.

Example: *The modern Olympic Games, they take place every four years, were first held in 1896.*

The modern Olympic Games, <u>which</u> take place every four years, were first held in 1896.

a   The house, which it was built in 1883, is now open for the public to visit.

....

b   First prize was given to Emily, whose short story impressed the judges.

....

c   Yesterday we met our new teacher, she is very interesting.

....

d   My neighbour, his car is bright yellow, has lived in that house all his life.

....

e   After the car park there is a supermarket, its opening hours are 24/7.

....

f   The football stadium, where we used to watch my favourite team play, has been destroyed in a fire.

....

g   Ahmed lives in Jeddah, where he likes very much.

....

h   The River Nile, which it is over 6500 km long, is Egypt's main source of water.

....

4   Choose a suitable word or phrase (A–H) to complete the sentences. Write the letter in the box.

A   where

B   which

C   which

D   which costs nearly $1000,

E   who lives in America,

F   who now lives in Portugal,

G   who went to the same school as me,

H   whose

a   Fabio's cousin, ☐ has two children.

b   My friend Francesca, ☐ has just started university.

c   My grandmother, ☐ was born in China.

d   We stopped at the museum, ☐ we had never visited before.

e   I've just come back from London, ☐ John lives.

f   Yesterday I met a woman named Susan, ☐ husband works in London.

g   He gave me the letter, ☐ I read immediately.

h   That laptop, ☐ is the best one available.

Challenge

5 Create complex sentences using an appropriate relative clause and making any other necessary changes.

Example: *Drinking plenty of water is a sensible thing to do. It keeps your body hydrated.*

Drinking plenty of water, which keeps your body hydrated, is a sensible thing to do.

a Keeping fit is a very important way to stay healthy. It should be done regularly.

....

b Michael went to university in London. He studied English Literature.

....

c Michael had to leave the university. He did not like his course.

....

d My grandfather is 75. He goes swimming in the lake every day.

....

e The car costs $150 000. It can reach speeds of up to 200 kph.

....

f These trousers only cost me $15. They are a lovely dark blue colour.

....

g Cyprus is an island in the eastern Mediterranean. Temperatures can reach more than 40 degrees in the summer.

....

h We heard about the World Scout Jamboree. This is an event arranged by the Scout organisation.

....

6 Choose **four** of the topics, organisations and people from the box. Write **two** sentences about each one. Each sentence should include a non-defining relative clause.

Example: *The modern Olympic Games, which are held every four years, take place during the winter and summer months.*

Guinness World Records	**the Olympic Games**
Guðlaugur Friðþórsson	**Iceland** **Param Jaggi**
the Scout organisation	**Soma Akriton** **volunteering**

....

....

....

....

....

....

....

Skills focus: Writing

1   Fill in gaps a–k in the following paragraph using words and phrases from the box.

> audiences   authoritative   balanced   for and against
> formal   format   informative   media   opinion
> persuade   readers

Articles often aim to **(a)** .... the reader about a certain topic, so they may be based only

on the writer's **(b)** .... – they will be one-sided. However, other articles may be more

(c) ...., offering ideas both **(d)** .... an argument or idea. Such articles invite the

reader to make up their own mind about something. Articles can appear in different **(e)** .... and

for different **(f)** ...., from school magazines to print newspapers to online articles, designed for

either adults or younger **(g)** .... When writing an article, it is important to consider your audience

and in what **(h)** .... your articles will appear. You want to sound

(i) .... and **(j)** ...., so most articles

should adopt a relatively **(k)** .... style.

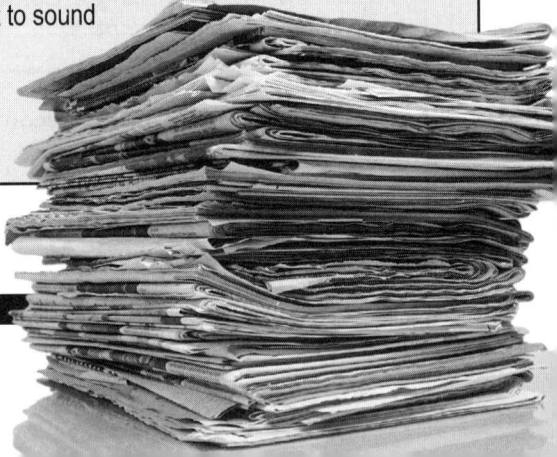

2 Draw lines between the parts to make complete sentences or explanations.

When you write, it is important to be aware of who is going to read your writing,	adjust the formality of your language accordingly.
You need to consider what your audience's expectations are and	as this will affect the words and expressions that you use.
Imagine you meet a new teacher, how would you greet them?	No doubt you would greet each of them differently, but why?
Now imagine you meet a good friend in the street,	What about a teacher you already know?
And then you meet a family member – how would you greet them?	what would you say?

3 Look at this writing task, then answer the questions.

A youth group you volunteer with has asked you to become a team leader. The local newspaper has asked you to write a short piece about the role for its community interest pages.

In your article, explain what the team leader role is and the activities that you need to organise.

Here are some comments from other team leaders:

Being a team leader means giving more personal time to help others.

It's about being creative and thinking about how to organise the group.

Now write an article for the local newspaper.

The comments above may give you some ideas, and you should also use some ideas of your own.

Write about 120 to 160 words.

a Who is the audience?..

b What level of formality is needed?...

c What is the purpose of the article? ....

d What type of argument is needed – persuasive or balanced?....................................

4 Read this student's response to the writing task in Activity 3, and the comments on how to improve it.

The organisation I volunteer with does different activities. We do this to collect money for different charities. It goes to charities that help people and to sports groups. We help people in different situations, in care homes and hospitals. Since I joined the group I've made some new mates. We meet even if the youth group does not.

The activities we do are different. Sometimes we wash cars or help clean up people's gardens. Last weekend I collected money for helping someone in their kitchen. My pal got paid for babysitting two kids. Another friend is really awesome on the guitar. He went to two different hospitals in town and played for some patients.

- Could include a title.

- Write a short introduction giving details about the youth organisation (including its name, location, etc.).

- Make the reason clear for writing the review, and your own position.

- Use a greater variety of language (avoid repetition of words such as 'different', 'collect money', 'we', etc.).

- Use more formal language (avoid informal phrases such as 'a lot of', 'awesome', etc.).

- Use more cohesive devices and longer, more complex sentences.

- Add a conclusion.

- This is 114 words, so make sure it is in the word range stated in the task.

Now rewrite the answer, using your notes to help you.

....

....

....

....

....

....

....

....

....

Writing, formal writing

The organisation you volunteer with would like to recruit more young people. Write an article for your school magazine encouraging other students to volunteer.

In your article, describe the work you do and the impact you have, and explain how students themselves can benefit from doing voluntary work of this kind.

Here are some comments from other young volunteers:

It's good to know you're doing something useful in your free time.

I've learnt things from doing this voluntary work that I don't think I would ever learn in school.

Now write the article, giving your views.

The comments above may give you some ideas, and you should also use some ideas of your own.

Write about 120 to 160 words.

You will receive up to 6 marks for the content of your article, and up to 9 marks for the language used.

[Total: 15]

> Unit 13: Success and fame

Vocabulary focus: Success and fame

1   Add the missing vowels to complete these **eight** words from Unit 13 in the Coursebook.

    a   __ mb __ ss __ d __ r

    b   __ w __ rd

    c   f __ r __ c __ __ __ s

    d   h __ n __ __ r

    e   pr __ __ s __

    f   pr __ l __ f __ c

    g   r __ t __ r __ m __ nt

    h   t __ rr __ t __ ry

2   Write the words from Activity 1 next to the correct definitions.

    a   very strong and forceful ....

    b   the act of stopping work, usually at a certain age ....

    c   a prize or an amount of money that is given to someone following an official decision

    ....

    d   an area of land, or sometimes sea, that is considered as belonging to or connected

    with a particular country ....

    e   to speak well of someone ....

    f   an acknowledgement or show of respect for someone or something

    ....

    g   producing a great number or amount of something ....

    h   a person who represents, speaks for, or advertises a particular organisation or group

    ....

3   Use the words from Activity 1 to complete these sentences.

    a   Carlos had the .... of meeting the city mayor.

b He was probably the most .... songwriter of his generation.

c The man next door has a .... temper!

d The teachers .... the students when they do well at school.

e She received an .... for her services to the community.

f She's a former .... to the United States.

g The lions avoid that part of the savannah – it's not their ....

h What is the normal .... age in this country?

4 Circle the best word from each pair in italics to complete the sentences.

a They produce 20 million tonnes of *home / household* waste each year.

b A *severe / sore* drought is expected this summer.

c Fish *struggle / stride* to survive when the water level drops.

d The earthquake *survivors / strikers* are all safe now.

e Are you feeling *frightened / frustrated* in your job?

5 Choose words from the box to complete the sentences. You will not need all the words.

glacier	gorge	gravel	mountains	mud	plain
river	sand dunes	slush	snow	valley	

a There was .... on the hilltops, but not in the ....

b The heavy lorries got stuck in the .... and could not move any further.

c That large mass of slowly moving ice is called a ....

d The streets were filled with dirty .... when the temperature rose again.

e We sailed down the ...., admiring the tall ....
in the distance.

f There are .... very close to the beach.

Language focus: Discourse markers showing contrast

Foundation

1   Use words from the box to complete the information about discourse markers.
    Do not look at the Coursebook.

example	contrast	phrases	clues	paragraphs	flow

Discourse markers are words or short **(a)** .... that help a writer structure a text, giving

(b) .... to the direction it will take. They link sentences and **(c)** .... to make

a text **(d)** .... clearly. Discourse markers can be used to show different types of connection,

including addition, **(e)** ...., result, time and comparison, but here we are looking at those used

to show **(f)** .... Some discourse markers are used at the start of the sentence and others in the

middle. For example: _Although_ she lived in Madrid for a year, my sister still doesn't speak Spanish. The weather

was terrible, _nevertheless_ the festival went ahead.

2   Complete the table using the discourse markers from the box. You can use any marker
    more than once. For gaps e–i, the discourse marker should start with a capital letter.

nonetheless	although	despite	however
even though	in spite of	nevertheless	

a	his young age,	he won first prize.
b	his young age,	he won first prize.
He won first prize,	**c**	his young age.
He won first prize,	**d**	his young age.
e	he was young,	he won first prize.
f	he was young,	he won first prize.
He won first prize.	**g**	he was young.

He won first prize.	h	he was young.
He won first prize.	i	he was young.

Practice

3   Use the discourse markers of contrast from the box to complete the sentences.
Some words will fit in more than once sentence, but you should use each discourse
marker only once.

> **nevertheless**   **although**   **despite**   **even though**
> **in spite of**   **nonetheless**

a   She quickly learned some basic expressions in French, ... she had
never been to France.

b   .... his young age, he came first in the competition.

c   .... she asked him to bring some food, he arrived without anything.

d   The wind was blowing very hard. ...., they managed to put up
the tent.

e   He came first in the competition, ... his young age.

f   They had never sailed in such rough conditions before; .... they
managed to get back safely to the coast.

4   Complete the following sentences containing discourse markers with your own ideas.

Example: *We needed to stop for petrol. However, we couldn't find a petrol station.*

a   Although they told us not to be late,...

b   I had saved my money to buy a new phone, even though...............................

c   Despite the excellent restaurant reviews, ...

d   She said we could choose any book we wanted. Nevertheless ....

e   In spite of being told not to cross the field, ...

Challenge

5   Underline the incorrect discourse markers of contrast in these sentences.
Write the correct discourse marker on the line.

Example: *Despite we had plenty of time, we still missed the bus.*   *Even though*

a   In spite of Valerie plays very well, she doesn't want to be in
the school team.   ....

b   Although the noise, we enjoyed the restaurant.   ....

c   The weather was terrible. Although we still decided to go
for a walk.   ....

d   Nonetheless Nico studied very hard, he did not get good
enough grades.   ....

e   Alan is a really great guitarist. Despite Anna is even better.   ....

f   Nevertheless we hadn't met before, we got on really well.   ....

6   Rewrite these sentences using the information in brackets. Use a different discourse marker
showing contrast for each sentence. For e and f, use your own ideas for the second clause.

a   It is a really expensive holiday. (going for two weeks)

....

b   They were both invited to the concert. (only one of them went)

....

c   The homework was very difficult. (took one hour)

....

d   She had just eaten a large dinner. (ate some ice cream)

....

e   The price of petrol has increased enormously.

....

f   She is frightened of horses.

....

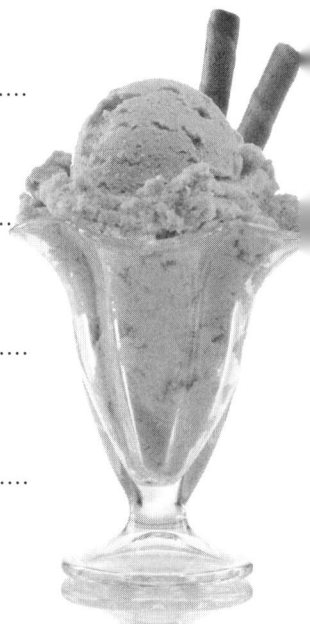

Skills focus: Reading

1 Use the words in the box to complete the text to find out about the man in the picture.

fastest	logged on	height	three	skydiver
	human	records	jump	

Felix Baumgartner: First person to freefall and break sound barrier

On 14 October 2012, more than eight million people **(a)** .... to YouTube to watch the Austrian

(b) .... Felix Baumgartner fall from a **(c)** .... of 39 km above the Earth.

His parachute **(d)** .... broke four world **(e)** ...., including the first

(f) .... to break the sound barrier in freefall and the **(g)** .... speed in freefall

(1357.64 kph) – and he did all this in only **(h)** .... hours.

---

2 The words in the box all appear in a newspaper article about Felix Baumgartner that you are going to read (Text 13.1). Use any resources available to check the meaning of the words, then fill in the gaps in the sentences.

aboard	cruising	drowned	feat	incidents
	leaping	soared	weeping	

a High in the sky they could see a .... passenger airliner.

b Many animals .... when the river flooded.

c The rescue services were called to several .... after the earthquake.

d The flight crew welcomed us .... the aircraft.

e Finishing all the housework in time was an amazing ....!

f He ran faster than anyone else, ... into first place and winning the race.

g The rocket .... into space, travelling at nearly 30 000 kph.

h The ending of the film was so sad that everyone was ....

3 The five paragraphs in the following newspaper article are in the wrong order.

Skim the article and write the numbers of the paragraphs in the correct order.

....

Text 13.1

[1] As well as becoming the first man to break the sound barrier unaided, Baumgartner set three other world records during the attempt. The first came after two hours and two minutes, when he broke the record for the highest manned balloon flight, breaking the record of Malcolm Ross and Victor Prather, who soared to 34 668 metres in 1961. Their record ended in tragedy when Prather drowned in the Gulf of Mexico upon landing.

[2] Coincidentally, Baumgartner's attempted feat also marked the 65th anniversary of US test pilot Chuck Yeager's successful attempt to become the first man to officially break the sound barrier aboard an aeroplane.

[3] He broke the current freefall record of 31.3 km held by Joe Kittinger. Mr Kittinger, who set his record in 1960, was the only person allowed to communicate with Mr Baumgartner while he was inside the capsule which carried him into space. As the launch began, Mr Kittinger told Mr Baumgartner: 'You're doing great, Felix. Doing great. Everything looks green and you are on your way to space.'

[4] Mr Baumgartner's parents were in Roswell, New Mexico for the launch, the first time they had travelled outside of Europe. His mother could be seen weeping as her daredevil son launched into space. While the action took place in the city of Roswell, famed for space-related incidents, attention was worldwide, with millions watching it online.

[5] Felix Baumgartner, a 43-year-old Austrian former military parachutist, floated for two hours in a purpose-built capsule towed by an enormous helium balloon before leaping into the record books from a height equivalent to almost four times that of a cruising passenger airliner. During the fall, he travelled at an average speed of 1357.64 kph.

Adapted from www.telegraph.co.uk/science

4 Answer these questions based on information in the text.

a What was Felix's job before he completed this freefall?

....

b What comparison is given about the height he jumped from?

....

c Who was Felix in contact with while he was in space?

....

d Why did Felix's parents travel out of Europe for the first time?

....

e What record was broken on the same day 65 years previously?

....

f What did Malcolm Ross and Victor Prather do in 1961?

....

5 Imagine you have decided to tell your classmates about Felix Baumgartner. First, you need to make some notes in order to prepare your talk. Look at these three headings and the three sample notes. Under which heading should each of the notes go? Write them in the correct place. Then write **two** more notes under each heading.

Travelled at 1357.64 kph

Mother seen weeping

43 years old

Background:

....

....

....

Family:

....

....

....

Achievements:

....

....

....

Reading, note-taking

Read the article about an architect called Kazuyo Sejima, and then complete the notes.

Text 13.2

Kazuyo Sejima

'Just what you'd expect from a Sejima building – lots and lots of glass,' was my first impression as I approached the Louvre-Lens. This incredible modern building in the small town of Lens in the north of France is an important art museum. It was designed by the Japanese architects Kazuyo Sejima and Ryue Nishizawa, who started the Tokyo-based architectural firm SANAA.

Sejima is regarded as one of the top architects in the world today, best known for her designs of public buildings rather than houses. Major projects outside Japan include a college in Essen in Germany, completed in 2006, and a theatre in Almere in the Netherlands in 2007.

While it would be wrong to say that Sejima's buildings all look the same, certain ideas influence all her work. She thinks very carefully about the visual connection between indoor and outdoor spaces, which is why large windows tend to be an important element in her buildings. When you're inside one of her buildings, you're very much aware of what's outside. She is also very concerned about how a building fits in with the surrounding area. In fact, she is said to take inspiration from the local environment. Some of her buildings, for example, consist mainly of square and cube shapes, while others are largely made up of curved walls. In 2013, a Sejima-designed factory for a furniture company in Germany was completed. The building is circular – an unusual shape in the manufacturing industry – and it can be divided into different sections allowing for production and storage to function at the same time. This is an example of another thing that Sejima tries to take into account in her designs: how people using the building might adapt it for different purposes.

Over the years, Sejima has won a number of awards for her designs and for buildings designed with Nishizawa. These awards led to other opportunities.

CONTINUED

For example, Sejima has been a judge for many international prizes. She has also taught architecture at universities in Japan and the USA, and, in 2010, she served as director of the 12th Annual International Architecture Exhibition.

In 2019, a major architectural project of a different kind was completed. Sejima and Nishizawa had been asked to redesign and restore a historic department store in Paris. In this project, as with her other work, Sejima focused carefully on the activities people are likely to carry out in the space. In particular, she was interested in the ways people might meet and communicate with each other. The new building has lots of shiny, smooth surfaces – another characteristic of Sejima's style – and is a very impressive sight in the heart of the French capital.

Imagine you are going to give a talk about Kazuyo Sejima to your class at school. Use words from the article to help you write some notes.

Make short notes under each heading.

Typical physical features of Sejima's buildings:

Example: a lot of glass

....

....

.... [3]

The main things Sejima considers when designing a building:

....

....

....

.... [4]

[Total: 7]

> Unit 14: Medical care

Vocabulary focus: Medical care

1   Which of these words are similar in meaning? Make **four** pairs. There are **two** extra words that you do not need to use.

hospital	patients	nurse	incident	treatment
dentist	paramedic	care	accident	casualties

....

....

2   Complete sentences a–h using the words from Activity 1. Definitions of the words are given in brackets.

a   A young man was involved in a violent .... yesterday. (unpleasant event)

b   A young woman was involved in a violent .... yesterday. (unexpected injury)

c   There were many .... on the hospital ward. (person receiving medical care and support)

d   There were many .... in the emergency department. (injured people)

e   The .... attended to the cases in her ward. (looks after people in a hospital)

f   The .... attended to the victims of the accident. (someone trained for medical work, not a nurse or doctor)

g   The .... for his illness was very thorough. (use of medicine to make someone better)

h   The .... given for his broken leg was very attentive. (giving what is needed to improve)

3 Match the words with the definitions. Write your answers in the grid.

a	b	c	d	e	f	g	h

a remedy	**1** cleanliness to prevent disease
b traditional	**2** upset or angry
c campaign	**3** change from one type to another
d offended	**4** a successful way of curing an illness
e infections	**5** a strategy or organisation designed to achieve an aim
f antibiotics	**6** medicine to destroy harmful bacteria
g hygiene	**7** conventional
h transition	**8** diseases in the body

4 Complete the sentences using **five** of the words from Activity 3.

a .... has an important role to play in avoiding getting ill.

b Scientists are sometimes cautious about .... medicine.

c A .... was set up to educate people about road safety.

d She was .... when she wasn't invited to the party.

e Certain types of tea are an effective .... for an upset stomach.

5 Complete the following table to show the different forms of the nouns listed.

Noun	Verb	Adjective	Adverb
accident			
campaign			
infection			
transition			
hygiene/hygienist			
vaccine/vaccination			
offender/offence			
breakthrough			

Language focus: Future in the past

Foundation

Remember that the 'future in the past' is a way of talking about the past but referring to something that was still in the future at the time. It uses past tense verb forms.

1 Draw lines to match the parts to make complete sentences. Underline the structure that shows the future in the past. The first one has been done as an example.

The surgeons expected that	take my temperature again in a few hours.
The last time I saw him,	the ambulance would be with us in five minutes.
The emergency services said that	the operation <u>would be</u> successful.
I saw the nursing accommodation that	I was to live in while I was training.
She said she was going to	the doctor was leaving to set up his own practice.

2 Circle the most appropriate structure to complete each sentence.

a I knew you . . . the exam – you didn't make any effort!

   would fail / are going to fail / will fail

b Sorry. I . . . you today, but I forgot.

   would visit / was going to visit / was visiting

c She asked if I . . . her, but there was nothing I could do.

   was helping / will help / would help

d I was very excited because tomorrow I . . . back home. Finally!

   was going / went / would go

e I asked them not to visit me that day because I . . . my final assignment.

   would be writing / wrote / was writing

f I . . . the dress, but then I decided I didn't really need it.

   was going to buy / would buy / was buying

Practice

3 Change the verbs in brackets into future in the past structures.

a They decided not to travel during the summer as they .... (plan) to redecorate the house.

b He promised he .... (send) a postcard from his travels.

c I .... (not go) plan anything for my retirement, but my husband encouraged me to.

d I couldn't go to the cinema because I .... (have) a meeting with my new manager.

e At the time, I thought we .... (go) together, but then my sister said she didn't want to come.

4 Circle the best words from each pair to complete the sentences.

a The teacher turned up late, just as the students *were about to / would* leave.

b I told Pietro that when he arrived at my place, we *would drive / were driving* to the shopping mall.

c Ahmed decided he *would go / will go* to his uncle's house.

d He applied for a different job because he *had planned / was planning* to leave.

e I promised I *would send / was sending* this letter yesterday, but I forgot.

f I knew you *would not ask / were not asking* about the homework.

Challenge

5 Tick (✓) the sentences that are correct. For any incorrect sentences, write the correct version on the line. In **two** cases, more than one answer is possible.

Example: *I didn't phone the doctor because I knew I saw her later.*

Incorrect: I didn't phone the doctor because I knew <u>I was going to/would see</u> her later.

a I would make a cake, but we'd run out of flour. ☐

....

b The movie would be over early, so can we eat after it finishes? ☐

....

c When we were passing the supermarket, we thought we'd stop and do some shopping. ☐

....

d   'Where's the kitchen?' 'It's down there. I thought Conrad will have shown you.'   ☐

....

e   The company's new management structure is to be announced tomorrow.   ☐

....

f   'The film was about to start, so shall we find our seats?'   ☐

....

g   He was driving far too fast and I thought he crashed the car.   ☐

....

h   I had already decided that as soon as I arrived in Italy I was ordering a pizza!   ☐

....

6   Rewrite these sentences, changing the time references. Turn the verbs into the future in the past form.

Example: *She has decided to go to university and she's leaving next week.*

She <u>had</u> decided to go to university and <u>was leaving</u> the following week . . .

a   We've agreed on the best place for our summer holiday and we're flying at the end of the month.

....

....

b   We're all very excited and can't wait to go.

....

....

c   My two cousins are coming with us and we are planning to meet them at the airport.

....

....

d I'm looking forward to trying out some different watersports, and my two sisters want to have a go at beach volleyball.

....

....

e I'm sure that my two cousins will be happy doing nothing all day long!

....

....

Skills focus: Listening and writing

1 You are going to listen to two people talking about their different experiences in nursing. One is a 'modern matron' and the other is a 'community nurse'. Which is which?

a Someone who cares for and treats people by visiting them in their homes.

....

b Someone who is in charge of other nurses in a hospital or clinic. Nowadays they are

called 'senior nursing officer'. ....

2 Listen to the people talking. For each question, tick the correct answer, A, B or C.

a The speaker became a matron because

A he loved working with elderly people. ☐

B he hated banking. ☐

C a family member inspired him. ☐

b He chose to specialise in mental health because

A he loved to be involved with his patients. ☐

B the patients don't wear uniforms. ☐

C he did a diploma in that area. ☐

c He became qualified to work in his present job by

A going to university and spending some time doing the course. ☐

B understanding how people's backgrounds influence them. ☐

C working in a private hospital. ☐

  d   People with mental health issues

      A   don't like going to work on Mondays. ☐

      B   have problems finding their way in life. ☐

      C   use their skills to get better. ☐

  e   The support community nurse

      A   was frustrated just looking after her child. ☐

      B   thought her children would be her lifelong career. ☐

      C   wanted nursing as a career. ☐

  f   In her first year as a qualified nurse

      A   she worked with patients who were very ill. ☐

      B   she was on her feet a lot. ☐

      C   she was rewarded for being organised. ☐

  g   After dealing with patients with cancer

      A   she worked in a hospital orthopaedic ward. ☐

      B   she visited places outside a hospital. ☐

      C   she only dealt with eight patients. ☐

  h   By working in people's own environment

      A   she makes them realistic about their illness. ☐

      B   she can test and educate patients. ☐

      C   she is aware of related conditions. ☐

3   An informal email is usually addressed to a family member or friend and contains details of a recent event that you experienced. Look at the task, then answer the questions.

You recently watched a documentary about the history of medical discoveries.

Write an email to a friend explaining what you saw.

In your email you should:

- explain why you decided to watch the documentary

- describe what you found out about the history of medical discoveries

- say which discovery you think is the most interesting or important.

Write about 120 to 160 words.

---

a What is the context? ....

b Who is the audience? ....

c What is the purpose? ....

4 Look at the jumbled sentences. Decide the best order for the sentences to create a response to the task in Activity 3. Look for clues in the sentences.

Dear Ziggy

How are you? Sorry for not replying sooner to your birthday wishes.

a For example, Harvey discovered the way blood flows around the human body as long ago as 1628!

b However, the most incredible thing for me was the use of robotic surgery, which is still quite young.

c I decided to watch it because I thought it would be useful for our science project.

d I want to update you about the medical discoveries documentary I saw last week.

e I was surprised to learn that not all discoveries in medicine are as recent as I thought.

f Instead of a team of doctors and surgeons, a single robot can carry out surgery, and with fewer risks to the patient.

g It's really amazing!

h Some of them go back hundreds of years.

i That should be the focus for our project.

j That's 400 years ago!

k What do you think?

Let me know soon so we can get started.

Miranda

Order: ....

5 Write your own response to the task in Activity 3. Use ideas from the Coursebook unit to help you.

....

....

....

....

....

....

....

....

....

....

EXAM-STYLE QUESTIONS

Listening, dialogue

You will hear eight short recordings. For each question, choose the correct answer, A, B, C or D, and put a tick (✔) in the appropriate box.

You will hear each recording twice.

1 What did the man find most challenging about training to become a nurse?

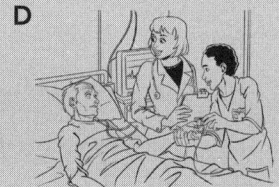

A □   B □   C □   D □ [1]

2 Where did the girl first notice that she wasn't feeling well?

A □   B □   C □   D □ [1]

3 What sport is the athlete going to compete in?

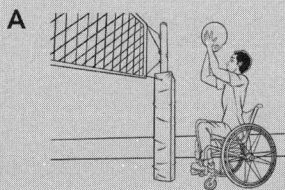

A □   B □   C □   D □ [1]

CONTINUED

4 What area of medicine does the student in training want to specialise in?

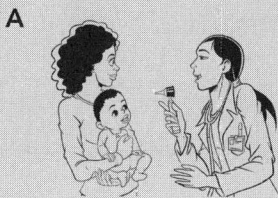

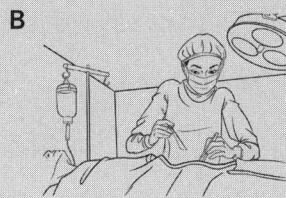

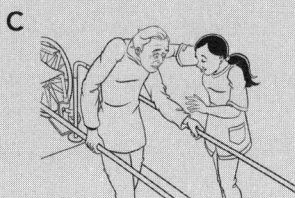

A   B   C   D

□   □   □   □ [1]

5 In which part of the body does the boy feel most pain?

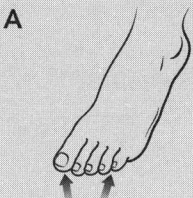

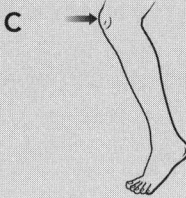

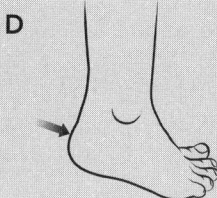

A   B   C   D

□   □   □   □ [1]

6 How did the girl raise money to buy new doors for her school?

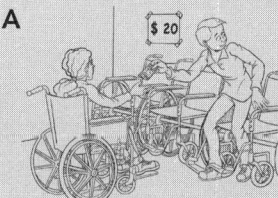

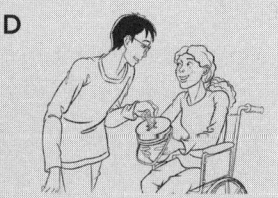

A   B   C   D

□   □   □   □ [1]

7 What issue will the paramedics discuss at the team meeting?

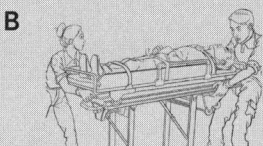

A   B   C   D

□   □   □   □ [1]

8 What is the medical student called Sara going to do next?

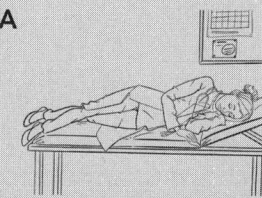

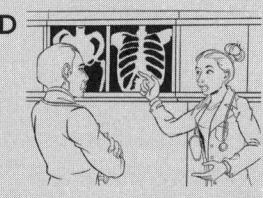

A   B   C   D

□   □   □   □ [1]

[Total: 8]

CONTINUED

Writing, informal writing

You were playing a game of basketball with some friends recently when one of them injured his leg.

Write an email to another friend, telling them what happened.

In your email you should:

- explain how the injury happened
- describe what you did to help your friend
- say how your friend is now.

Write about 120 to 160 words.

You will receive up to 6 marks for the content of your email and up to 9 marks for the language used.

[Total: 15]

....

....

....

....

....

....

....

....

....

....

....

....

> Unit 15: Healthy lifestyles

Vocabulary focus: Healthy lifestyles

1 Complete the crossword puzzle using words from Unit 15 in the Coursebook.

Across

2 Relating to the enjoyment or study of beauty (9)

3 Extreme tiredness (7)

5 Groups of similar things that are close together (8)

7 To gather in crops once they have finished growing (7)

8 To become weak and dry, and slowly fade away (6)

9 Indicating a longer distance away (6)

Down

1 First in order of importance (9)

2 Made a pain less severe (10)

4 An improvement or increase in something (5)

6 Something rare or expensive that is good to eat (8)

2 Complete these sentences using the words from Activity 1.

a The new hospital is quite ugly and its design has little

.... appeal.

b In some parts of the world this food is considered a ....

c The new medicine .... the pain in her back.

d Look at those .... of flowers, all in different colours.

e Farmers are reporting a very poor .... this year, due to the bad weather.

f The heart is the .... organ in the human body.

g Energy drinks can give a .... to athletic performance.

h Eating a banana during training can help prevent ....

i We export our products as far .... as Australia.

j Too much strong sunlight causes plants to ....

3 Here are **eight** more words from Unit 15 in the Coursebook. Put vowels in the gaps to complete the words.

a fl __ __ r __ sh __ d

b r __ __ d __ ng

c sc __ rc __ ty

d t __ xt __ r __

e __ d __ pt __ t __ __ n

f fl __ sh

g s __ ppl __ m __ nt

h wr __ nkl __ d

4 Choose **five** words from Activity 3 and use them in sentences of your own.

....

....

....

....

....

Language focus: Quantifying phrases

Foundation

1   Use the words and phrases in the box to complete the information about quantifying phrases. Do not refer to the Coursebook.

how much	**how many**	**uncountable nouns**	**before nouns**
too many	**noun**	**modify**	**information**	**adjectives**
	too much or *too many*		

Qualifying phrases are words and phrases that we use **(a)** .... in order to

(b) .... them. As with **(c)** ...., quantifiers give us extra

(d) .... about the **(e)** .... Quantifying phrases tell us about the quantity of

something: **(f)** .... (with countable nouns) or **(g)** .... (with uncountable and abstract nouns).

We use **(h)** .... + noun to mean more than we want or need of something. We use

(i) .... before countable nouns and *too much* before **(j)** ....

2   Use *much* or *many* to complete the sentences. Remember that *much* is used for a singular noun and *many* is used for a plural noun.

a   There weren't .... things for us to choose from.

b   .... elderly people live alone.

c   How .... free time do you have?

d   Please try not to spend too .... money.

e   Giovanni is worrying too .... about tomorrow's test.

f   How .... dollars do you have on you?

g How .... did you pay for that book?

h He has too .... problems and not enough solutions.

i She is in so .... trouble after being late for school again.

j They have been to .... concerts.

Practice

3 Look at these sentences from the audio you heard in Unit 15 in the Coursebook. Choose a quantifying phrase from the box to complete each sentence. In some cases, more than one answer is possible.

> a sufficient amount of   a few   one of
>
> a smaller number   a mix of

a .... different fruit and nuts is ideal, but even these should only be eaten in moderation.

b Did you know that not getting .... sunlight can have a negative impact on your health?

c Lastly, try eating .... of sugary treats.

d I saw a programme on TV .... days ago which explained that it is essential to spend time outdoors when the days are shorter.

e Last week I wanted to join a yoga class at my gym, instead of .... my usual dance lessons, but the club asked me to pay extra for it.

4 Circle the most suitable quantifying phrase in each pair to complete the sentences.

Example: *I'm afraid the brown sandals are sold out but we've got a few / a little pairs left in white.*

a The doctor told me to try eating *a smaller number of / not many* full meals every day.

b *Not many / Not much of* these tips will help you.

c We don't have *many / much* biscuits left but we have *a variety / a few* cakes available.

d Have you seen our new range? We don't have *many / much* of the old styles now.

e *One of the / Some of* the cars in the museum is 100 years old.

f Can I have *a few / one of the* minutes of your time to talk about this?

Challenge

5 Use any suitable quantifying phrase except *too much* or *too many* to complete these sentences.

a There are .... cakes to choose from, but you're only allowed one.

b Can I have .... more ice cream please?

c Only .... of people came to the exhibition.

d We voted on the school trip and .... students chose the museum.

e The new menu contains .... of food for vegetarians.

f The hotel garden looked amazing, although .... the flowers had started to wither.

6 Write **six** sentences of your own using the quantifying phrases in the box.

the majority of	a minority of	a number of	plenty of
a few minutes of		a mix of	

....

....

....

....

....

....

Skills focus: Reading and speaking

1 You are going to read a text called 'Dealing with asthma triggers'. Before you read, use any reference sources available to complete the two sentences below:

a *Asthma* (noun) is ....

b *Triggers* (plural noun) means ....

2 Skim the text, then add sub-headings to sections A, B and C. Choose from:

- Coping with common triggers
- What is a trigger?
- Common asthma triggers

Text 15.1

Dealing with asthma triggers

A ....

[1] People with asthma have what's called a chronic or continuing problem with their airways (the breathing tubes in their lungs), which are swollen and full of **mucus**. This problem is made worse by asthma **triggers**, such as animal hair, exercise or smoke.

[2] Triggers are substances, weather conditions or activities that are harmless to most people. But in people with asthma they can lead to coughing, **wheezing** and shortness of breath. Triggers don't actually cause asthma (no one knows exactly what does cause it), but triggers can lead to asthma symptoms.

B ....

[3] Triggers include:

- colds or the flu
- allergens (things that cause allergic reactions, such as animal hair and plant pollen)
- irritants in the air (such as perfume, smoke and air pollution)
- weather conditions
- exercise

C ....

[4] Allergens are one of the most common asthma triggers. Allergens include mould, dust, cockroaches and pollen. Animal fur or feathers can also trigger asthma. If you think you might have an allergy, talk to a parent or doctor about getting allergy tested.

[5] In addition to other treatments for allergies, doctors recommend avoiding allergens. It isn't possible to avoid everything, of course, but there are some things you can do:

- Keep your room as clean and dust free as possible – that means vacuuming and dusting weekly and getting rid of clutter. Your old teddy bears may need to go into a box in the attic!

- Wash your sheets weekly in hot water and get rid of feather pillows and comforters. You can get covers for your mattress and pillows that will help too.

- Get rid of carpets and curtains. Rugs, carpeting and other heavy material can trap allergens that make you ill.

[6] Irritants are different from allergens, because they can also affect people who don't have allergies or asthma. Irritants don't create a serious problem for most people, but for those with asthma they can be a trigger. Common irritants include perfumes, aerosol sprays, cleaning products, smoke, paint or gas **fumes** and air pollution. Even things that may seem harmless, such as scented candles, are triggers for some people.

[7] If you notice that a household product triggers your asthma, ask your family to switch to an unscented or non-spray version of it. If smoke bothers you, a fire or woodstove can be a problem.

[8] If outdoor air pollution is a trigger for your asthma, running the air conditioner can help. You can check air-quality reports on the news to monitor which days might be bad for you. Then, on days when the quality is especially bad, you can stay in air-conditioned comfort, whether it's at your house or the mall.

Adapted from http://kidshealth.org

3 Answer the questions about the text.

a What and where are the 'airways'?

....

b What actually causes asthma?

....

c What advice is given for people who think they might have an allergy?

....

d How are irritants different from allergens? Give an example of each.

....

....

e What should someone do if a household product triggers asthma symptoms?

....

f According to doctors, what can be done to avoid allergens? Give **four** pieces of advice.

....

....

....

....

4 Imagine that your teacher has asked you to complete a presentation about asthma, and has given you two options as the focus of the project:

- asthma triggers
- allergens and irritants.

Choose **one** of the options and prepare some written notes about it, using Text 15.1 for information. Then prepare a short, spoken presentation. When you are ready, audio or video record yourself delivering the presentation and share it with some of your classmates. Listen to or watch their presentations and give them feedback using these criteria:

- What does each student do well?
- What could each student improve on?
- How does this relate to your own speaking skills?

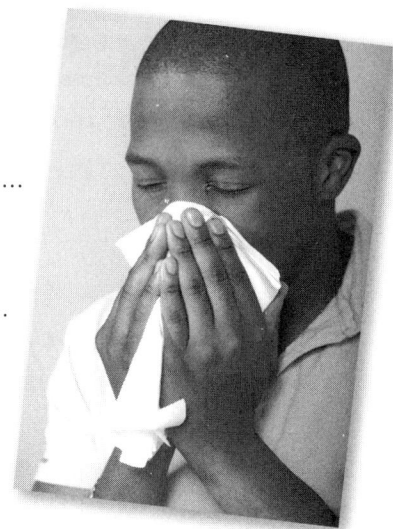

EXAM-STYLE QUESTIONS

Reading, open response

Read the article about a weekly running event called Parkrun, and then answer the questions.

Text 15.2

Parkrun

It's 9 o'clock on Saturday morning and I'm standing at the starting line of my local Parkrun, just as I've done on many other Saturday mornings. Today, there are 106 **participants** ready to take on the 5-km course, which is essentially two laps of the park. Some will race round it, others will jog and a few will just walk. The youngest is nine years old and the oldest is 88. Because of an ankle injury, I can't run at the moment, so instead I'm a volunteer in charge of checking runners' barcodes at the start of the run; when it's over I'll be processing the runners' times.

My regular venue is a local park, but in the last eight years I've done Parkruns through a nature reserve in Australia, a forest in Germany and on a beach in Ireland, among other locations. I still have a very clear memory of my first Parkrun. I remember thinking 'this isn't as difficult as I imagined' as I jogged around a beautiful lake with a group of other runners. I was very keen on sports as a teenager, but I let things slip as an adult. Then, just after my 30th birthday, I started doing Parkruns and, within a few weeks, I found I'd lost some weight and felt much fitter.

The first ever Parkrun was held in October 2004. It was organised by a keen **amateur** runner called Paul Sinton-Hewitt. On the first Saturday that the race was organised, 13 people ran 5 km around Bushy Park in west London and Sinton-Hewitt timed them doing it. The thinking behind the choice of 5 rather than 3 or 10 kilometres was that it was both achievable for beginners and challenging enough for experienced runners.

The Saturday run became a regular event and before long, more people started attending. Then, other runs were established across the UK, and then around the world. They all use the same simple process: you register on the Parkrun website, download and print a barcode, turn up to an event 15 minutes before it starts, then complete the run and receive your time. Today, every Saturday morning, 6 million people turn up and run in 2000 different locations, supported by 500 000 volunteers, in 21 countries around the world.

What is it that attracts so many people to do Parkruns? It doesn't hurt that the whole experience is free, of course. It's also open to everyone; it's hard to imagine a more diverse group of people than the participants in my local Parkrun.

CONTINUED

I still see new people joining my local run every week, and there seems to be no shortage of commercial sponsors willing to pay for new events, the Parkrun website and the salaries of the small team of full-time staff that manage the organisation. Also, there appears to be no end of volunteers ready to take on various duties: setting out the course, supervising safety, and so on. Parkrun looks as though it's here to stay.

Glossary

participants (noun): people who do an activity with other people

amateur (adjective): doing something as a hobby

---

1   Where did the writer take part in their first Parkrun?   [1]

   ....

2   Why did the founder decide that the run should be 5 km long?   [1]

   ....

3   How many Parkrun events take place each week worldwide?   [1]

   ....

4   Give **one** reason why the writer thinks that Parkrun is very popular.   [1]

   ....

5   Where does the money to pay for Parkrun come from?   [1]

   ....

6   What responsibilities do Parkrun volunteers have? Give **three** details.   [3]

   ....

   ....

   ....

[Total: 8]

CONTINUED

Speaking, short talk

Look at speaking card A on the topic of keeping fit. You have one minute to read the card and prepare, but you cannot write any notes.

Using the ideas on the card, give a short talk to a partner. (If you're doing this at home, try recording your talk instead.) Your short talk should last 2–3 minutes.

When you finish, change roles and listen to your partner giving a short talk using speaking card B.

Card A

Keeping fit

You are planning to do more exercise in your free time. You are considering the following options:

- joining a local gym

- taking up jogging outdoors.

Discuss the advantages and disadvantages of each option. Say which option you would prefer, and why.

Card B

Keeping fit

You are planning to do more exercise in your free time. You are considering the following options:

- doing dance classes together with your friends

- riding a bike in your local area.

Discuss the advantages and disadvantages of each option. Say which option you would prefer, and why.

> Unit 16: Animal life

Vocabulary focus: Animal life

1 Match each word a–h with one of the groups of words. Then circle the word in each group that is the closest synonym.

a nocturnal (adjective)

conduct	attitude	look	style

b habitat (noun)

feed	gain	nurture	develop

c endemic (adjective)

intricate	simple	splendid	beautiful

d cultivate (verb)

late	night-time	dark	daytime

e elaborate (adjective)

native	original	home	domestic

f venture (verb)

say	progress	rest	go

g macabre (adjective)

scary	disturbing	pretty	ugly

h behaviour (noun)

street	locality	house	territory

2 Use words a–h in Activity 1 to complete this text about lions. In some cases, you may need to change the form of the word.

Lions are often considered to be kings of their territory. As lions are **(a)** .... animals they are rarely seen during the day. Lions tend to be more active when it is cooler, and their excellent night vision can be six times more sensitive to light than humans. This gives them a huge advantage at night when other animals **(b)** ....

into the lions' **(c)** ...., which it is their role to defend.

Lions communicate through a range of different **(d)** .... Surprisingly, they perform many peaceful actions, such as licking each other and rubbing heads. They also vocalise with each other to show affection or aggression, depending on the sound. All of these movements are

very **(e)** .... Lions are mostly **(f)** .... to parts of Africa, where

they have **(g)** .... a very relaxed lifestyle. During the day the male of the species tends to lie around in the shade for 16 to 20 hours, waiting for the first

food offerings. A **(h)** .... fact about lions is that they are able to eat about 8 kg of meat a day – equivalent to a human eating about 70 burgers!

3 Write the words from the box next to the correct definition.

> dominance (noun)   versatility (noun)   intrigue (verb)
> endangered (adjective)   judge (verb)   squirt (verb)

a an ability to easily change from one thing to another ....

b at risk of being harmed or lost ....

c the quality of being more important or stronger than something else

....

d to force liquid to flow out suddenly ....

e to have or give an opinion about something ....

f to interest someone a lot ....

4 Choose the correct word from Activity 3 to complete the sentences.

a People love their pets because they feel animals don't .... their character or behaviour.

b Several animals, such as octopuses and some insects, can .... poison to kill their prey.

c Some animal behaviour can .... zoologists.

d It is important that the male lion maintains its .... in the family group.

e Some animals are no longer .... thanks to conservation and breeding programmes.

f Many animals show .... and are able to adapt well to their environment.

5 Use a different form of the word in brackets to complete these sentences.

a The area was not fit for .... (habitat) because of the flooding danger.

b Constant .... (cultivate) of the land had emptied the soil of all nutrients.

c The behaviour of some types of wildlife is particularly ……………………….. (intrigue).

d The attempt at ……………………….. (dominate) by the two organisations had become a fierce competition.

e Finally the ……………………….. (judge) came through and the animals' natural habitat was saved.

f ……………………….. (potential) the law may need to change, but the government has not decided yet.

Language focus: Adjectives with nouns

Foundation

1 Underline the adjectives in A and B.

A Nobody has to worry if they look different.

B Clothing is made in a rushed manner.

a Which sentence has an adjective before a noun?

b Which sentence has an adjective after a verb?

2 Underline the adjective in each of these sentences about the clothing industry. Then say if it comes before a noun or after a verb.

a Current fashions determine clothes production. ……………………………………………………

b This has a harmful effect on the environment. ……………………………………………………

c The fashion industry appears stable, showing no signs of slowing down. …………………

d The methods used were more precise than the ones used in the industry today.

……………………………………………………………………………………………………

e New styles are created almost weekly. ……………………………………………………………

f A reduction in the quality of clothing seems inevitable. ……………………………………

g It is not only poor quality that encourages people to throw out their clothes. ……………

h Countless chemicals are used in the production process. …………………………………

Practice

3 Complete these sentences using the adjectives in the box.

> adorable   attentive   bewildered   comfortable
> supportive   helpless   inquisitive

    a All the kittens were ………………………. but the children could choose only one.

    b The students were very ………………………. and interested in the experiment.

    c The hotel was very ………………………. with everything supplied by the

        ………………………. staff.

    d The teachers were very ………………………. and gave their students confidence.

    e They were ………………………. by the amount of detail that was required to complete the form.

    f The animal caught in the trap was ………………………. and fighting for its life.

4 Rewrite each of these sentences so that the adjective comes before a noun. Remember to use a relative pronoun or linking word in your rewritten sentences.

Example: *The results from students in Year 10 look <u>great</u>.*

Students in Year 10 got <u>great results</u>.

    a The rainy season has been <u>awful</u> this year.

    ………………………………………………………………………………………………………

    b Her laugh was <u>nervous</u> when she was uncomfortable with a question.

    ………………………………………………………………………………………………………

    c The price he quoted for the work was <u>outrageous</u>.

    ………………………………………………………………………………………………………

    d The families were <u>worried</u> when they heard the news about the accident.

    ………………………………………………………………………………………………………

    e The late breakfast meant that the start to the day was <u>unusual</u>.

    ………………………………………………………………………………………………………

Challenge

5 Make adjectives from the words in the box. Then use the adjectives to complete the sentences.

> use   comfort   ~~danger~~   help   pain   suit

Example: *The road was very <u>dangerous</u> after the heavy rains.*

a He sat on the ……………………….. sofa, and settled in for the evening.

b She found having her tooth out fairly ……………………….. despite the anaesthetic.

c His friend felt ……………………….., as he refused to accept any help.

d The company couldn't find a ……………………….. candidate to fill the new job.

e The instructions were very ……………………….. and she was able to build the furniture easily.

6 Make your own complete sentences using the adjective and noun provided.

a angry / mob

………………………………………………………………………………………………………

b bored / students

………………………………………………………………………………………………………

c comfortable / furniture

………………………………………………………………………………………………………

d dull / weather

………………………………………………………………………………………………………

e enthusiastic / participants

………………………………………………………………………………………………………

f filthy / bedroom

………………………………………………………………………………………………………

Skills focus: Reading

1 Look again at the text about lions in Vocabulary Activity 2. Find and underline **four** facts about lions.

Example: _more active when it is cooler_

2 Think of **four** animals that you are familiar with and write **one** fact under these headings.

Animal	Food	Size	Characteristics and behaviour	Habitat

3 Read Text 16.1, then answer the questions.

Text 16.1

Insects are not so bad!

[1] Insects are just about everywhere. The biological class of _insecta_ includes everything with six jointed legs: ants, bees, flies, beetles and many more. An insect's body is made up of three parts: head, thorax and abdomen. All insects also have two antennae on their heads, which they use for smelling, feeling and, in some cases, even listening. All the insect species are divided into 32 groups. The largest of these is for beetles, which has about 500 000 species!

[2] To the best of our current scientific knowledge there are about one million different insects on Earth, representing 90% of all life forms. However, some scientists believe that the total number of insect species could be ten times that number, so there are still plenty to be discovered.

The main reason for the success of insects is their size, which makes it easy for them to hide from hunters such as birds and other animals. Being small also means that an insect's energy requirements are fewer than for larger creatures. In addition, many insects have wings – a fast way to reach safety, or search for food or mates. A further reason for the success of insects is that many will happily eat both natural and artificial foods. Lots of insects feed on plants while some prefer to eat other insects. Mosquitoes prefer blood, while a few insects such as cockroaches and ants will eat crumbs off the kitchen floor.

[3] One of the best-known insects is the hardworking ant. Although it is impossible to know for sure, some scientists estimate that there

---

are close to 1.5 million ants for every human on the planet! You will find ants both outdoors and indoors, although not in Antarctica, the one place on Earth where it is too cold for insects to thrive. In addition, the majority of insects cannot survive in seawater, and therefore our oceans are mostly free of these creatures.

[4] Even though we tend to think of insects as being small, some are actually pretty big! On your travels you may come across the South American longhorn beetle, which can be as long as 25 cm (about the same as a rat). The African goliath beetle weighs up to 100 grams, and there is a huge female stick insect that can be nearly 40 cm long! But while ants, beetles, flies and cockroaches may annoy us, they perform many important ecological roles. Insects pollinate flowers and plants, which allows the plants to reproduce. Insects also produce honey, silk and wax. Some insects eat dead animals, and others are beneficial as predators. Insects are really not so bad!

Paragraph 1

a What does the word *jointed* mean? Do humans have jointed legs?

....

b Find **three** features that all insects have.

....

c Which senses are *not* mentioned?

....

Paragraph 2

a What is the most important reason for the success of insects?

....

b How many different reasons are given for the success of insects?

....

c Give an example of artificial food.

....

Paragraph 3

a Which word has a similar meaning to *guess*?

....

b Which insects does the text say are not found in Antarctica?

....

c Replace *In addition* with a word with a similar meaning.

....

Paragraph 4

a What does the word *tend* mean?

....

b Which word means *very large*?

....

c Why is it so important for humans to accept insects?

....

EXAM-STYLE QUESTIONS

Reading, multiple matching

Read the article about four people (A–D) who have studied zoology. Then answer questions a–i.

Text 16.2

A Aisha Murphy

For the past three years, I've worked on a sloth conservation project in Costa Rica. It's amazing this is what I've ended up doing because I grew up on a dairy farm in Northern Ireland and my parents were very keen for me to study agriculture. My interest was always in wild animals, though, so it was hardly unexpected that I did a zoology degree. The first two years of the course gave students a broad understanding of the subject, although my personal preference was to study animal behaviour rather than biology – some of that is very challenging. I spent the third year doing research at the sloth project where I'm now employed, and I learnt a huge amount about sloths and how to do research. I also learnt how to think for myself and solve problems, both of which are crucial in many different careers.

B Callum Bond

It's often assumed that zoology students just want to be zookeepers, but actually only a few end up working in zoos. There are many different directions we can go in, including jobs that have very little to do with animals. Having said that, I feel very lucky because ever since I was small, I've always dreamt of being a zookeeper and that's my job now!

My teachers warned me that I might not achieve this aim, and they were right to do so because zoos rarely have jobs available, and when one comes up lots of people apply. What helped me was that during my degree, I did a six-month work placement in a zoo. I enjoyed the whole of my degree, but I must say that the best part was my time at the zoo.

C Grace Chan

I'd always been interested in the natural world, but my science teacher said that while a zoology degree might be fun, he doubted whether it would lead to a secure job. So, I went for computing. After a year, however, I felt I was wasting my time and managed to switch to zoology, which I absolutely loved. The best part was the final year when we all had to do a research project. I wanted to investigate how a recent plan to clean up a local river might affect either fish or frogs that lived in it. For ages, I was in two minds about which to focus on, but I eventually chose the fish. After working on the project for three months, I realised that the aims I'd set myself were impossible to achieve in the time I had, so I had to think about things differently. But I learnt a huge amount from doing it.

D Paolo Gomes

Most people think the typical zoology student is passionate about whales, tigers and other well-known wildlife – and they're probably right. My great passion, however, is for insects, especially ants and beetles. I've long been concerned about the drop in the numbers of many insect species, but they tend to get ignored by conservation programmes. One of the reasons I studied zoology was so that I could make a more effective contribution towards insect conservation. Fortunately, my university tutors gave me plenty of guidance and support – even though what I wanted was often rather different from most other students! I now work as a researcher for an organisation that gathers data on insects and does what it can to persuade national and local governments to introduce insect-friendly environmental policies.

For each statement, write the correct letter A, B, C or D on the line.

Which person

a   says skills developed during their course are useful for work unrelated to zoology?   .... [1]

b   admits to having had unrealistic ambitions at one stage?   .... [1]

c   appreciates the attention paid to their individual needs?   .... [1]

d   refers to the difficulty of finding work in their chosen field?   .... [1]

e   says it was predictable that they would study zoology?   .... [1]

CONTINUED

f	regrets following some advice they were given?	.... [1]
g	admits that they found one aspect of the subject hard to understand?	.... [1]
h	is keen to make people aware of the problems facing particular types of wildlife?	.... [1]
i	mentions a common misunderstanding about people who study zoology?	.... [1]

[Total: 9]

Reading, multiple choice

Read the article about a project to protect sheep from attacks by a type of wild cat called a puma, and then answer the questions.

Text 16.3

Protecting sheep and saving pumas

Helen Gray visits a ranch in southern Chile where people are trying new ways of protecting sheep from pumas.

Estancia Cerro Guido is a huge ranch on the edge of Chile's Torres del Paine national park. It is a centre for adventure tourism, offering hiking, mountain biking and horse-riding across the wide grasslands and in the spectacular mountains nearby. But, with 20 000 sheep, it is a traditional ranch too, and, like other ranches in the region it has a problem with pumas – or mountain lions as they are also known. Since sheep farming was established in southern Chile 150 years ago, pumas have attacked sheep, and ranchers have hunted pumas to prevent their sheep being killed. Although hunting pumas has been illegal in Chile since the 1980s, it still happens. In fact, wildlife organisations claim that the government deliberately ignores it because it provides employment for local hunters, as well as protecting the sheep.

Recently, however, there has been a rise in 'predator tourism': tourists visiting the area in the hope of seeing pumas in the wild. And ranches have taken the opportunity to make money by providing 'puma observation packages', which include tours by guides skilled at tracking down these beautiful but shy creatures. Conservation organisations, including Panthera, a charity that tries to protect all types of wild cat, have noted how ranchers who were killing pumas just 10 years ago, now regard them as a key part of the history and culture of the region.

But pumas are still hunted and killed. Many ranchers are badly hit by the loss of sheep to these wild cats. <u>At least</u>, that's the way the ranchers see it. In a recent survey,

---

45 ranchers from the region said pumas were responsible for 19% of their annual sheep losses. That's a significant amount. But when researchers looked into the data, they found that the actual losses were less than 1%. While some ranchers may lose more animals than others to pumas, there does appear to be a gap between belief and reality.

In the last few years, an interesting partnership has developed between the owners of Estancia Cerro Guido and the wildcat conservationists at Panthera. The aim of the project is to experiment with new ways of keeping pumas away from the sheep without hunting them.

One plan has been to install 'Foxlights' around the ranch. Designed by an Australian farmer to keep foxes away from his chickens and lambs, Foxlights are solar-powered, multi-coloured lights that flash in the dark with the aim of frightening the pumas away from flocks of sheep.

Special dogs called maremmas have also been introduced. For centuries, these have been used by shepherds in Italy to protect their sheep against wolves. Before I first saw these dogs at Estancia Cerro Guido, I had read that they live with sheep from a very young age so they develop a strong, protective relationship with them. What I hadn't imagined was how closely maremmas, with their fluffy white fur, match the sheep in both size and appearance. Since the dogs were first brought to the ranch, a 30% drop in sheep killings has been reported.

So, are these ideas likely to make much difference to the complicated relationship between ranchers and pumas? Conservationist Laura Gomez, who has been involved in developments at Estancia Cerro Guido, told me that if the project is successful, it may encourage other ranchers to adopt similar measures. She has also noticed something about the area around the ranch: pumas there appear to be going back to their old food sources – wild animals like rabbits and guanaco – rather than sheep. That's good news for the natural ecosystem.

1   The writer suggests that the law protecting pumas is

   A   not strictly enforced.   ☐

   B   no longer necessary.   ☐

   C   out of date.   ☐   [1]

CONTINUED

2 In paragraph 2, the writer suggests that local attitudes towards pumas have changed because of

    A   pressure coming from environmental organisations.   ☐

    B   a reduction in the number of times they are seen.   ☐

    C   economic benefits associated with them.   ☐   **[1]**

3 The writer uses the words 'At least' in paragraph 3 to emphasise that   ☐

    A   certain claims made about puma attacks may be incorrect.   ☐

    B   farmers' experiences of damage caused by pumas vary a lot.   ☐

    C   local people know more than anyone else about the risks posed by pumas.   ☐   **[1]**

4 What is the writer doing in paragraph 5?

    A   introducing a new subject   ☐

    B   presenting a contrasting idea   ☐

    C   giving more detail about a point made   ☐   **[1]**

5 What surprised the writer about the dogs he saw at the ranch?

    A   how similar to sheep they looked   ☐

    B   how effectively they seemed to do their job   ☐

    C   how quickly they had adapted to a new place   ☐   **[1]**

6 How does a conservation expert the writer spoke to feel about the project?

    A   unsure whether it could be copied elsewhere   ☐

    B   optimistic about its impact on the environment   ☐

    C   concerned about the lack of attention it receives   ☐   **[1]**

[Total: 6]

Vocabulary focus: The environment

1 Complete the crossword puzzle using words from Unit 17 in the Coursebook.

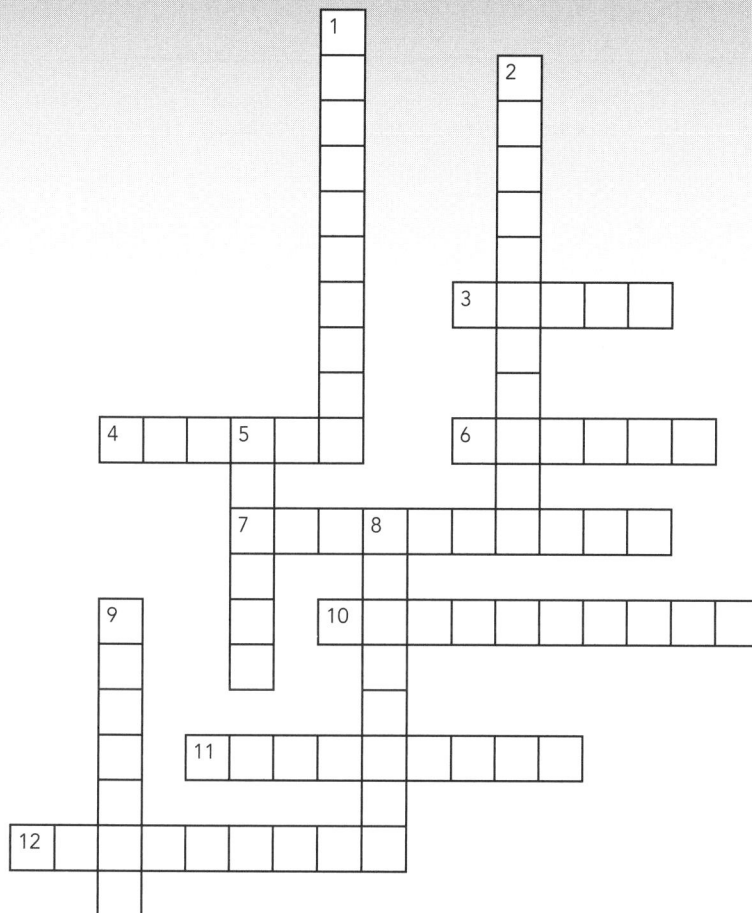

Across

3 Part of a large country, with its own government (5)

4 A particular area or part of the world (6)

6 To make something certain to happen (6)

7 Buying (10)

10 The characteristic of believing that good things will happen in the future (9)

11 A large landmass usually made up of several countries (9)

12 Almost (9)

Down

1 Plants in general (10)

2 Promises or decisions to do something (11)

5 A consequence or effect (6)

8 The total amount that can be contained or produced (8)

9 An independent part of the world, with its own government (7)

2 Complete the sentences using the words from Activity 1.

a After washing the shirt several times, the ink stain has .... disappeared.

b Asia is the largest .... and Australia is the smallest.

c I don't agree with your negativity. I feel very .... about the situation.

d Luxembourg is a member .... of the European Union.

e That area will have to be cleared of all the overgrown .... if we want to use it for sports.

f The Basque .... is situated in the northern part of Spain.

g The campaign has had a major .... on young people.

h This department is responsible for .... everything the company needs.

i The stadium has .... for 75 000 fans.

j The whole .... celebrated a national holiday.

k All countries must honour their .... to protecting the environment.

l To .... that nobody gets lost, everyone should download the map app.

3 Complete the text below using the correct form of **eight** words from Activity 2.

> The environment is everything around us. It can be living, such as **(a)** .... and animals, or non-living, such as water and chemicals. Many scientists do not feel **(b)** .... about the future of our planet. They feel that **(c)** .... should make more of a **(d)** .... to dealing with environmental issues, to **(e)** .... a secure future for Earth. We know that climate change has had a dramatic **(f)** .... on people's lives, and in some **(g)** .... farming has **(h)** .... stopped due to a lack of water.

4 Look at these definitions of **five** more words from Unit 17 in the Coursebook. Fill in the missing letters to identify the words.

  a a group of countries or people that have similar political interests: b __ __ __

  b able to be easily physically hurt, influenced or attacked: v __ __ n __ __ __ __ __ e

  c involving a lot of thought, skill and effort: a __ __ __ __ __ __ __ s

  d made by joining separate parts together: as __ __ __ __ __ __ d

  e to reduce or limit something: c __ __ t __ __ __

5 Write **five** sentences of your own using the words from Activity 4.

....

....

....

....

....

Language focus: Reference words

Foundation

1 Choose words from the box to complete the information about reference words. There are **two** extra words that you do not need to use.

adjectives	back	content	links	previously
	pronoun	repetition	sentence	

A reference word is a word that looks **(a)** .... and connects to a word, phrase or an idea that has

(b) .... appeared in a text. Reference words are important because <u>they</u> not only help the writer

to avoid **(c)** ...., but they also help the reader to understand the **(d)** .... of a

text. For example, in this paragraph the **(e)** .... *they* (underlined) refers back to *reference words*.

All types of pronouns (for example, *I*, *mine* and *that*) as well as possessive **(f)** .... (for example,

my, *her*) can be used as reference words.

2   Circle the most suitable reference word from each pair to complete the sentences.

a   Look at *that / this* car over there. It's *mine / my*.

b   Can *our / I* borrow *my / your* umbrella? *I / you* think it's going to rain.

c   'There are six apartments in *this / that* building over there. *They / That* all have three bedrooms.'

   'All of *they / them*? *Those / Them* two on the top floor don't look large enough.'

d   Can you try *this / its* for me? I'm not sure if I like *its / it* taste.

e   I visited *those / my* grandparents last weekend. *Their / My* new house is really lovely.

Practice

3   Use the reference words from the box to fill in the gaps in the first paragraph of an article about beaches. For each reference word, draw an arrow to show what it links back to. The first one has been done as an example.

> it   their   their   them   these   they
>
> they   this   we   ~~you~~

Beaches are good for everyone and everything!

[1] Even if you live hundreds of kilometres away from a beach, (a) (you) will know that beaches play an important

part in our lives. Not only do (b) .... use (c) .... for leisure activities, but

(d) .... also help to reduce the damaging effects of storms and winds, which benefits people

living near the coast and (e) .... communities. Furthermore, beaches provide habitats for different

vegetation and animal life, many of which rely on organisms buried in sand. (f) .... play an
essential role in 'cleaning' seawater and in providing food for larger creatures, such as birds and turtles. Some

mammals need a beach free of pollution for (g) .... own relaxation (including sunbathing!)
as well as for breeding and giving birth. In order for a beach to support all of this life,

(h) .... has to be clean and safe, and that is
why your involvement is so critical. Without

(i) ...., beaches will become more

littered than (j) .... already are.

4 Re-read the Language tip about introductory phrases in Section B of the Coursebook. Start each of the following sentences with an appropriate introductory phrase and say what structure it is followed by.

Example: . . . *we're too late.*

It looks as though *we're too late. (verb phrase)*

a .... a nesting turtle.

b .... completely free of rubbish.

c .... that beach has been cleared of rubbish.

5 Write **three** more sentences of your own. In each sentence, underline the introductory phrase and say what structure it is. Use a different introductory phrase in each sentence.

....

....

....

Challenge

6 Now fill in the gaps in the second paragraph of the article about beaches using appropriate reference words of your own choice. Draw arrows to indicate what each reference word is referring back to. The first one has been done as an example.

[2] Beach pollution is not just about beachgoers who fail to take home **(a)** their plastic bags, bottles and cans. Every year, our beaches are used as rubbish tips for everything from old bicycles to car tyres.

(b) .... are health hazards not only for those of us who regularly use beaches, but also for the creatures that rely on **(c)** .... for food and shelter. Incredibly, humans have caused some beaches to be covered with up to 30 cm of plastic, and still **(d)** .... complain about **(e)** .... being dirty. Due to the movement of the oceans, plastic in the water is constantly being broken down. **(f)** .... becomes smaller and smaller until **(g)** .... even becomes airborne. A few years ago, a dead whale was found with nearly 6 kg of plastic inside **(h)** .... stomach, which probably caused the whale's death.

Skills focus: Reading and writing

1   Look back at paragraph 1 of the article. Circle the best sub-heading for this paragraph.

   • Beach pollution kills!

   • Our beaches are alive!

   • Vegetation and plastic

   • Being close to water

2   Now look back at paragraph 2 and choose the best sub-heading from the list.

   ....

3   Skim paragraph 3 of the article. Write your own sub-heading for this paragraph.

   ....

Text 17.1

[3] Around the world, volunteers regularly clean up beaches, making shores safer and much more pleasant places to visit. More importantly, removing pollution from the ocean and coastal ecosystems ensures that marine life can thrive. Furthermore, volunteers can collect information about the types of rubbish that are causing pollution. This information can be used to investigate how to reduce specific rubbish from ending up in our oceans and on our beaches. As an example, the use of plastic drinking straws has been dramatically reduced in recent years. This resulted from videos of birds trying to eat the straws, mistaking them for food. Beaches need the help of volunteer cleaners!

Read the article about the importance of keeping beaches clean, and then complete the notes.

Imagine you are going to give a talk at your school about the importance of beaches.
Use words from the article to help you write some notes.

Make short notes under each heading.

The importance of beaches:

Example: beaches used for leisure activities

   ....

   ....

   ....

> **Problems and solutions for pollution:**
>
> ....
>
> ....
>
> ....
>
> ....

4   Read the third paragraph of the article again, then look at the note-taking task that follows.

   Now look at these notes, which a student has made about the text. In each box, write the paragraph (1–3) where the information can be found.

   a   dangerous for animals   ☐

   b   used for lesiure activities   ☐

   c   birds eat plastic such as straws   ☐

   d   reduce effects of weather and sea on people's lives   ☐

   e   volunteers clean up our beaches   ☐

   f   clean-up can tell us about differnt types of pollution   ☐

5   Write the notes under the correct heading in the task in Activity 4.

6   Re-read the article and find **one** more piece of information to add to each sub-heading.

7   Use your notes to write a report for your teacher about the importance of beaches.

   In your report, you should explain how important beaches are, talk about the dangers that pollution creates, and suggest how we can help.

   Write about 120 to 160 words.

   ....

   ....

   ....

   ....

   ....

   ....

   ....

....

....

....

....

....

....

....

EXAM-STYLE QUESTIONS

Reading, note-taking

Read the article about the increase in the use of micromobility vehicles, like bicycles and scooters, in many towns and cities, and then complete the notes.

Text 17.2

Micromobility vehicles

Recently, there have been important changes in the way people move around the towns and cities where they live and work. One particularly obvious trend is the increased use of micromobility vehicles: bicycles, e-bikes, scooters, electric scooters, electric skateboards, roller skates and so on.

These vehicles can be either human powered or electrically powered, although the latter is increasingly common. If you watch people travelling around on these vehicles, there is one obvious attraction: they're fun to ride! One reason for this is that they enable the rider to avoid heavy traffic. Another common sight is not so positive, however: these vehicles are often left abandoned in public places – something that many people complain about.

What specific features make a vehicle fit the category of micromobility? Firstly, they have a maximum weight of 500 kg (although many vehicles weigh much less than that). They should also have a top speed of 45 kph, though most rarely go that fast.

There is no doubt that in some places the popularity of micromobility vehicles is growing fast. In Europe, there are now over 20 million e-scooter users,

CONTINUED

and the market might be worth as much as 100 billion euros by the end of the decade. The fact that the costs involved in owning or renting them are relatively low is significant, especially among younger people. Also, maintaining them is usually quite straightforward.

These vehicles are also popular with politicians, planners and urban experts, who see them as a solution to some of the biggest issues that cities face today. They work well with public transport systems: an e-scooter, for example, may be the best way of getting from home to the nearest train station, or from a bus stop to home at the end of the day. And when people travel through a city on these small vehicles rather than in cars, it significantly reduces pollution.

Any major change in the way people move around urban areas is unlikely to be completely problem-free, of course. Safety is a major concern, particularly with so many new users. The best way to deal with this, according to experts, is to consider how we lay out our city streets. Many towns and cities don't have enough lanes reserved for bicycles and other micromobility vehicles. This means that people ride on pavements, competing for space with unhappy pedestrians, or on normal roads surrounded by heavy traffic. There are, of course, many laws about owning and driving a car, but micromobility vehicles do not yet have any similar laws to govern their use. In many countries, this issue needs to be dealt with urgently.

Imagine you are going to give a talk about micromobility vehicles to your class at school. Prepare some notes to use as the basis for your talk.

Make short notes under each heading.

Arguments in favour of using micromobility vehicles:

Example: fun to ride

....

....

....

.... **[4]**

CONTINUED

Challenges presented by the increased use of micromobility vehicles:

....

....

.... [3]

[Total: 7]

Writing, formal writing

Your headteacher wants to reduce the number of students travelling to and from school by car.
They have asked you to write a report on the issue.

In your report, outline the reasons why there should be a reduction in the number of car journeys to and from school, and suggest how other ways of travelling could be made more attractive to students.

Here are some comments from other students in your school:

The roads in the area
around the school are
always very busy.

The buses only
come every
30 minutes.

Now write a report for the headteacher.

The comments above may give you some ideas, and you should also use some ideas of your own.

Write about 120 to 160 words.

You will receive up to 6 marks for the content of your report, and up to 9 marks for the language used.

[Total: 15]

....

....

....

....

....

....

CONTINUED

> Unit 18: Feeding the world

Vocabulary focus: Feeding the world

1 Here are the definitions of **six** words from Unit 18 in the Coursebook. Work out the words then add them to the table. What extra word is made in the vertical grey column?

   a   to buy something

   b   to eat something

   c   needing or using great energy or effort

   d   a long period with little or no rain

   e   causing little or no damage to the environment

   f   deserving trust; dependable

Extra word: ....

2 Choose the best word from Activity 1 to complete each sentence.

   a   If there's another ...., none of our crops will survive.

   b   For a few weeks, they followed an .... English course.

   c   It is not .... to keep taking water from underground sources.

   d   We need a more .... system for transporting farm produce.

   e   People .... more food now than ever before.

   f   You must .... a ticket before you get on the train.

3 Here are **ten** more words from Unit 18 in the Coursebook. Add vowels to complete the words.

a p __ st __ c __ d __ s

f m __ scl __

b s __ bst __ t __ t __

g c __ ntr __ b __ t __

c b __ __ t __ chn __ l __ gy

h f __ rth __ rm __ r __

d c __ ll

i s __ t __ sfy __ ng

e r __ v __ l __ t __ __ n __ ry

j thr __ __ t __ n __ d

4 Circle the incorrect words in sentences a–h. Write the correct word above the incorrect one. All the words are from Activity 3.

a A muscle is the smallest basic part of an animal or plant.

b We need to substitute more to helping other people.

c The farm is very productive. Unfortunately, it also provides plenty of employment opportunities.

d Nowadays, it is possible to contribute real meat with alternative types of food.

e It is very intensive to know that all our hard work was successful.

f Some rainforests are more revolutionary than others.

g Sometimes we need to use satisfying techniques to solve problems.

h The use of cells to change food growth is unacceptable to many people.

5 Choose **six** words from Activity 3 and use them in your own sentences.

....

....

....

....

....

....

Language focus: Noun phrases

Remember that a noun phrase is a group of words made up of a noun along with the words used to describe it. Noun phrases can come either before or after verbs.

Foundation

1   Match the phrases to make complete sentences. Write the letter of the second half of the sentence in the box next to the first half. The first one has been done as an example.

   a   Many foods that we grow damage   [F]

   b   Farming processes in many parts of the world are   [ ]

   c   Some foods that harm the planet are   [ ]

   d   More than 145 million tonnes of sugar (sucrose) is produced   [ ]

   e   Sugar production uses   [ ]

   f   One of the most common ingredients in fast food is   [ ]

   g   The use of chemicals damages pests, but it also affects   [ ]

   h   Rice farming can be made   [ ]

   i   Fast-food outlets also use   [ ]

   j   Many fast-food products have to be   [ ]

   A   the entire ecosystem.

   B   always going to be popular.

   C   improving.

   D   less wasteful by switching to more efficient means of irrigation.

   E   a lot of packaging.

   F   our planet.

   G   transported long distances.

   H   meat.

   I   per year in about 120 countries.

   J   water intensively for irrigation.

2 For each statement in Activity 1, circle the main verbs and underline the noun phrases that come before and after the verb.

Example: _Many foods that we grow_ (damage) _our planet._

Practice

3 Complete these sentences using the noun phrases in the box.

> Even young children   ~~Learning to cook~~   Most people
> School cooking classes
> The number and variety of restaurants in our town
> The ways in which food is sold, prepared and cooked

Example: . . . _should be part of every school programme._

Learning to cook should be part of every school programme.

a ………………………............... will benefit from compulsory cooking classes at school.

b ………………………............... provide children with a possible career route.

c ………………………............... accept that these classes will be useful for children of all ages.

d ………………………............... has changed dramatically in the last 50 years.

e ………………………............... has risen considerably.

4 Draw lines from the noun phrases on the left to make complete sentences.

Those houses at the end of the street	all live in the same street.
These six young children	are very old.
At the concert a boy wearing a blue shirt	is a friend of mine.
The woman who served us in the shop	is from Italy.
The boy we met in the restaurant	sells the most amazing cakes!
The bakery in the shopping mall	was sitting in the front row.

Challenge

5 Complete sentences a–h with any suitable noun phrase using the nouns in brackets.

Example: *(scientists) . . . predict a continued increase in the global population.*

<u>*Many scientists around the world/Scientists who study population growth*</u> *predict a continued increase in the global population.*

a (the boy) .... took all the food that was left.

b (researchers) .... believe that poverty will increase in the future.

c (farmers) .... are able to help the environment.

d (technology) .... can help us to live more economically.

e (science) .... has been responsible for saving many lives.

f (fires) .... destroyed houses and made many people homeless.

g (restaurants) .... provide different ethnic food choices.

h (programmes) .... are shown in several different channels every day of the week.

6 Add your own words to make more descriptive noun phrases.

Example: *The man bought the car.*

The <u>tall, elderly man from the house opposite</u> bought the <u>old</u> car <u>from his neighbour.</u>

a The girl never drinks milk.

....

b They played basketball.

....

c Giacomo loves fishing.

....

d My grandparents never travelled abroad.

....

e My cousin used to eat meat.

....

f The car turned a corner.

....

g Katerina took a photo.

....

h He made a phone call.

....

Skills focus: Writing

1 Read this writing task, then answer the questions.

Your class recently visited a biotechnology laboratory. Your teacher has asked you to write a report on what you saw.

In your report, say what you learnt from the visit and give your opinion about using science to help produce more food.

Here are some comments from other students in your class:

> We should be thankful for biotechnology, as it makes sure we produce enough food to eat.

> It was a good chance to meet experts.

> I won't touch food that is full of chemicals – it's the same as poisoning myself.

> There wasn't enough time to do anything practical.

Now write a report for your teacher.

The comments above may give you some ideas, and you should try to use some ideas of your own.

Write about 120 to 160 words.

---

a Who is the audience? ....

b What is the context? ....

c What is the purpose? ....

2 Look at these three introductory sentences written by students in response to the task. Tick (✓) the one you think is most effective. Then create an introductory paragraph by adding **at least two** ideas that could follow on from the sentence. Remember – you need to *introduce* the topic and give your *opinion* about it.

    a Personally, I think governments should spend more money on biotechnology research so that the world will always have enough food. ☐

    b The visit to the biotechnology laboratory provided us with an enormous amount of information about scientific food production. ☐

    c There is nothing we can do about the global food shortage, but science can help. ☐

....

....

3 Look at these three concluding sentences. Tick (✓) the one you think is the most effective. Then create a concluding paragraph by adding **at least two** ideas that could follow on from the sentence. Remember – you need to *restate your opinion* about the topic, and bring the report to a natural close.

    a In conclusion, and taking into consideration all the different arguments, my firm belief is that we should thank science. ☐

    b On the other hand, there is already enough food so we should share it out more equally. ☐

    c Another point is that food and science do not mix, so let's eat natural food. ☐

....

....

4 Now write the body of the report. Think carefully about how many paragraphs you need in order to express your opinions, and remember the word limit. You can use the comments from other students, but also try to use some ideas of your own. Include a title and sub-headings if you want to.

....

....

....

....

....

....

....

....

....

....

....

EXAM-STYLE QUESTION

Writing, formal writing

You recently listened to a podcast on the subject of whether it is better to buy food that is produced locally rather than food that is imported from other countries. You decide to write an article on the subject for your school magazine.

In your article, you should say whether or not people should mainly consume locally produced food, giving reasons for your views.

Here are some comments you heard on the podcast:

The further food has to travel, the less tasty and nutritious it is likely to be.

International trade is important for all sorts of reasons.

Now write an article for your school magazine.

The comments above may give you some ideas, and you should also use some ideas of your own.

Write about 120 to 160 words.

You will receive up to 6 marks for the content of your report and up to 9 marks for the language used.

[Total: 15]

....

....

....

....

....

CONTINUED

> Unit 19: Lifestyles

Vocabulary focus: Lifestyles

1 Complete the crossword puzzle using words from Unit 19 in the Coursebook.

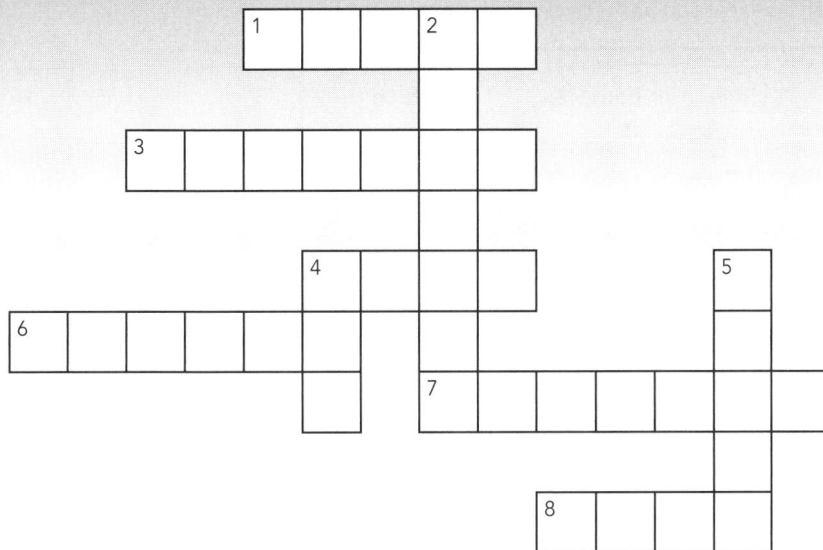

Across

1 A supply of something (5)

3 Everything the same (7)

4 To look carefully or with difficulty (4)

6 The level of sound produced (6)

7 A sports shoe (7)

8 A colloquial word for clothing (4)

Down

2 Belonging to the present time (7)

4 A domesticated animal (3)

5 To emphasise how important or powerful something is (5)

2 Look at these definitions. Each one is an alternative meaning for one of the words from Activity 1. Write the word next to the definition.

Example: *A person who coaches others* trainer

a flow of electricity ....

b controls the speed in a car ....

c to stroke an animal ....

d clothes worn by students at school ....

e something to add flavour to food ....

f a person of the same age ....

g extremely steep ....

h the amount contained within an object ....

3 Replace the underlined word or phrase in each sentence with a word from the box.

> | ~~merchandise~~   wages   circle   complex   absolute |
> | inferior   obstacles |

Example: *People complained about the quality of the <u>goods</u> in the shop.* merchandise

a I have <u>total</u> faith in her judgement. ....

b It is a very <u>complicated</u> problem with no easy solution. ....

c These products are <u>poor</u> compared to the ones we had before. ....

d There were too many <u>difficulties</u> blocking our progress. ....

e My <u>salary</u> stayed the same, but I benefited from customers' tips. ....

f My <u>group</u> of friends got much bigger when I went to university. ....

4 Circle the most suitable word from each pair to complete these sentences.

a The *inspiration / fascination* for my story is my childhood home.

b Some plants are more *tolerant / passive* to high temperatures than others.

c Everything was dealt with very *suspiciously / openly* and we were happy with the result.

d I lived far from other people and felt very *isolated / impacted*.

e He was a *fearless / frightened* player who attacked without thinking about his own safety.

5 Add a suffix from the box to these words. Say what part of speech each word is. Make any necessary spelling changes.

Example: *fortune + -ate = fortunate (adjective)*

> | -ly   -ity   -ism   -ate   -ful   -ic |

a professional + ... = ...

b different + ... = ...

c   success + ………………………. = ………………………..

d   hygiene + ………………………. = ………………………..

e   responsible + ……………………… = ………………………..

Language focus: The position of adjectives

Remember that adjectives are used to add descriptive detail. They can be positioned either before a noun or after certain verbs (*be, seem, look, become, appear, sound, taste, feel, get*).

Foundation

1   Write the adjectives from the box in the correct categories in the table. Add **two** more adjectives of your own to each category. One has been done as an example.

young	amazing	square	small	blue	cooking
new	purple	metal	huge	ancient	running
green	oval	ugly	exciting	tiny	triangular
	glass	school	woollen		

Opinion	Size	Age	Shape	Colour	Material	Purpose
		young				

2   Use **two** adjectives from the table to complete each sentence, using the adjective types in brackets.

a   She was carrying a very ……………………….. , ……………………….. bag. (size and colour)

b   They have some ……………………….. , ……………………….. paintings. (opinion and age)

c   He bought a ……………………….. , ……………………….. hat. (material and purpose)

d   Look at that ……………………….. , ……………………….. table – very strange! (shape and colour)

e   There's a really .... , ... design on my new shirt.
    (opinion and colour)

f   The university has a .... , ... collection of books
    in the library. (size and age)

Practice

3   Use **two** adjectives to complete each sentence. You can use adjectives from the previous two
    activities, or choose your own.

a   The .... , ... ships were found under the water.

b   A(n) .... , ... car was found abandoned in the park.

c   While it was snowing, they climbed the .... , ... track.

d   A(n) .... , ... man walked into the room and sat down.

e   The children played all day with a(n) .... , ... video
    game they had been given.

f   The plates on the table were .... and ....

4   Choose words from the box to complete the sentences. Use the hints in brackets to help you.

> | contemporary | traditional | business-like | mandatory |
> | fashionable | personal |

a   Something that must be done by law is .... (A . . . prison sentence.)

b   If your clothes are up-to-date, then you are .... (She wears . . . clothes.)

c   If an issue concerns only you and is not public, then it is ....
    (This is a . . . issue.)

d   When you have a professional approach to your work, you are ....
    (A . . . person.)

e   If you are conventional and use long-established practices, then you are

    .... (A . . . practice.)

f   Anything modern, such as art and fashion, is also known as ....
    (A . . . art exhibition.)

Challenge

5 Add **one** adjective from the box under each verb in the table. Note that some adjectives can go with more than one verb. Then write sentences using the verb + adjective combinations.

Example: *Everyone in the team just wants to <u>be better</u> next season.*

delicious	beautiful	soft	faster	tired
complicated	unhappy	~~better~~		

~~be~~	seem	look	become	appear	sound	taste	feel
~~better~~							

....

....

....

....

....

....

6 All these sentences contain a verb followed by an adjective. Underline the verb and the adjective in each sentence. Rewrite each sentence so that the adjective comes before a noun.

Example: *The reviews of the school play <u>were fantastic</u>.*

The school play got <u>fantastic reviews</u>.

a All the fans in the stadium appear nervous.

....

b The food in the school canteen tastes awful.

....

c That street musician sounds amazing!

....

d Wearing new clothes always makes me feel fashionable.

....

e Having so many different pairs of shoes seems excessive to me.

....

f Everybody gets distracted by things that are unexpected.

....

Skills focus: Reading and listening

1 The words in the box all appear in Text 19.1 – an article called 'Alone on an island'. Write each word next to its definition.

> solitary   authorities   disaster   donated
>
> caretakers   sculpting   designated   landed

a an event causing great harm or suffering   ....

b arrived somewhere from the sea   ....

c creating something from wood or other materials   ....

d alone, not with others   ....

e gave money to others   ....

f government officials   ....

g people employed to look after a place or thing   ....

h given a particular purpose   ....

2   Skim the text and use the words from Activity 1 to fill in gaps a–h.

Text 19.1

Alone on an island

[1] Mauro Morandi's decision to sail to the South Pacific in 1989 ended in what seems like

(a) .... His **catamaran** broke down off the west coast of Italy, between the islands of Sardinia and Corsica. But rather than returning home, Morandi's life changed forever

when he (b) .... on the small island of Budelli, considered one of the most beautiful islands in the area and famous for its *Spiaggia Rosa*, or Pink Beach. At the time, a couple had been living there as the island's

(c) .... for several years. Luckily for Morandi, they had just decided to retire, and he saw an opportunity to begin a new type of life there.

[2] In 2016, Budelli was (d) .... as a National Park and since then the Italian

(e) .... have been asking Morandi to leave so that they can transform the island into an educational centre. While tourists are able to visit the island by boat during the day, the beaches are off-limits, and swimming is not permitted.

[3] Even though Morandi lives alone on the island, his lifestyle is certainly not lonely, as tourists visit daily. Using solar energy for power, he has access to social media and the news to keep him up-to-date with the world beyond the island. His lifestyle is not boring either, as he keeps himself

busy (f) .... wood and then selling his designs to tourists. All the money he

collects is (g) .... to charities around the world. He also spends a lot of time reading and taking photographs of the island's plants, seascapes and sunsets. Any visitor who wants to know more about the island's ecosystem will find that Morandi's years living on Budelli have taught him everything there is to know.

[4] Morandi, now in his early 80s, says he does not want to return to city life after more than

30 years living as a (h) .... islander, but he has no choice. He had hoped to spend the rest of his life on the island he called home, but now he is moving to a small apartment on the island of La Maddalena, which is the largest in the area. With a population of around 11 000, Morandi certainly will not feel lonely, and he says that because he will still be able to see the sea, his lifestyle will not change too much.

Glossary

catamaran (noun): a type of boat with two floating sections

3   Which of the following sub-headings matches which paragraph in the text? Write the paragraph number in the box. There are **two** extra sub-headings that you do not need to use.

a   An artistic lifestyle   [ ]   d   The chance of a lifetime   [ ]

b   No time to get bored   [ ]   e   Too many people   [ ]

c   Only a small change   [ ]   f   Visit and learn   [ ]

4   Read the text more closely and answer these questions.

a   Why did Morandi stop on the island of Budelli?

....

b   Who was living on the island when Morandi landed?

....

c   Why does Morandi need to leave the island?

....

d   Where does Morandi get electricity from?

....

e   Why will Morandi not feel lonely on La Maddalena?

....

f   What does Morandi do to keep himself busy? Give **three** details.

....

....

....

5   What do the following fashion-related words mean? Use any reference sources available to help you write a definition for each word.

a   fibre ....

b   spin ....

c   thread ....

d   weave ....

e   cloth ....

6 Look at the image of the jacket. Where are the hood, collar and pocket flap? Label them.

7 You are going to listen to an interview with a designer who is helping to manufacture a range of jackets with mobile-phone and MP3 technology. First, read the questions and underline the key word(s) in each one. Then listen and answer the questions.

a What has changed about clothing over the years?

....

b How many basic stages are there in the clothes-making process?

....

c What roles do the three partners have?

....

d Where in the new jackets will the earphones be?

....

e What will happen when the phone rings?

....

f How are the phone and the MP3 player controlled?

....

g Where does Conte get the ideas for his clothes from?

....

h   What type of garments form the majority of Conte's collection?

....

i   What does Conte hope to include in his future designs?

....

j   Name **two** benefits of face-recognition cameras.

....

....

k   Why do you think the interviewer asks if Conte's designs will look fashionable?

....

EXAM-STYLE QUESTIONS

Reading, open response

Read the page from the website of a travel blogger called Lucy Moore, and then answer the questions.

Text 19.2

Lucy Moore – travel blogger

My name's Lucy Moore, I'm 35 years old and for the last ten years I've travelled the world and written about what I've seen and done. My spirit of adventure was inspired by my grandfather, who visited 47 different countries when he worked on ships. Listening to his stories, I decided that one day I'd match his total. I began travelling when I was 25 and within five years, I'd been to 45 different countries. I've now managed 72, and my plan is to get to 100.

Initially, whenever I went to a new country, I'd visit as many different places as possible in the limited time I had. These days, I stay in one location for longer; rushing around has lost its appeal. Also, my budget isn't so tight, so I book better accommodation than I could afford ten years ago. Having somewhere quiet makes it easier for me to write articles for travel magazines or any of the other things I do to pay for my travels.

My highlights of the last year include: riding a camel across the Sahara Desert, which was incredible; visiting beekeepers in Slovenia and writing about them for a guidebook (I quite often get paid to contribute specialist sections to guidebooks); and acting in a

CONTINUED

film in India. I had a tiny role, but it was the most unusual few days of the whole 12 months for me!

During my first year travelling, I lived off savings I'd made when working for a software company. The skills I acquired in that job have since proved very useful too. Not only have I created my own website, but I now help other bloggers design their sites, and that brings in some useful cash. As my savings ran out, I looked for other ways to finance my new lifestyle, and realised that once my blog had gained a certain number of followers, I could get companies to advertise on my website – and charge them for it.

I'm currently based in northern Malaysia. I was asked by a publisher to edit some books for teenagers and it's the kind of work I can do anywhere. I'm also blogging and taking photos of the wonderful street food here. When I started travelling, my photography was very basic, but I've worked at it and I'm quite proud of the pictures I take now. That's more than can be said for my language learning. I was hoping to pick up some Malay while I'm here, but sadly, as I've experienced elsewhere, I've had limited success.

I have a few plans for the coming months. I'm visiting a friend in an area of Japan I've never been to before. Then, I'm off to Tonga in the South Pacific, where I'll be diving with whales. That'll be a first for me, and I can't wait. After that, I'm cycling along the west coast of Canada with a cousin of mine. What an interesting life I lead!

1   How many countries did Lucy originally aim to visit?

    .... [1]

2   What does Lucy do now that is different from when she first started travelling? Give **one** detail.

    .... [1]

3   What does Lucy say was the strangest experience she had in the last year?

    .... [1]

4   What does Lucy wish she was better at?

    .... [1]

5   What is Lucy most looking forward to doing in the coming few months?

    .... [1]

CONTINUED

6 What does Lucy do to make a living? Give **three** details.

....

....

.... [3]

[Total: 8]

Listening, multiple matching

You will hear six people talking about fashion.

For each question, choose from the list (A–H) which idea each speaker expresses. For each speaker, write the correct letter (A–H) on the answer line. Use each letter only once. There are two extra letters that you do not need to use.

You will hear the recordings twice.

Now look at the information A–H.

Information

A I design most of the things I wear.

B I dislike having to wear a school uniform.

C I get fashion ideas by following celebrities.

D I think being fashionable isn't very important.

E I feel under pressure to wear the latest brands.

F I get loads of inspiration from fashion magazines.

G I don't mind wearing the same trends as my friends.

H I only wear fashion that doesn't damage the environment.

1 Speaker 1 .... [1]

2 Speaker 2 .... [1]

3 Speaker 3 .... [1]

4 Speaker 4 .... [1]

5 Speaker 5 .... [1]

6 Speaker 6 .... [1]

[Total: 6]

> Unit 20: Technology and the future

Vocabulary focus: Technology and the future

1 Complete the puzzle using the words in the box. What is the new word under the arrow?

shorten	phenomenon	dock	inconvenience
neglect	evaluated	principles	isolation

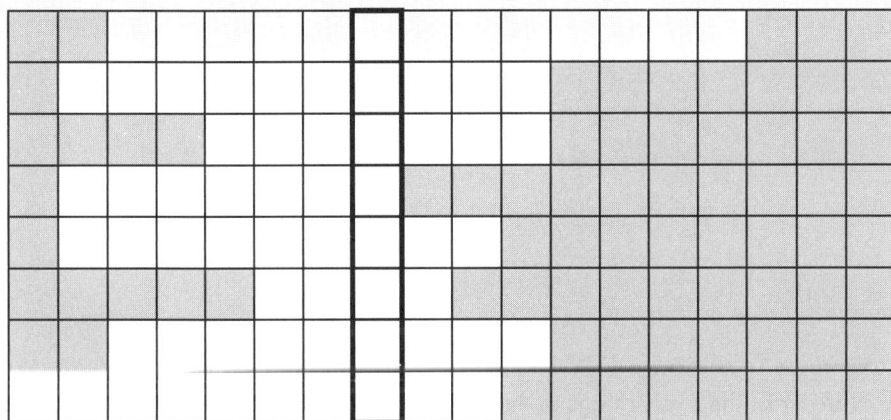

2 Use the **six** words in the box to complete the sentences.

battery	transmitted	runway	comparable	detached	cover

a The island's small airport .... was not suitable for large aircraft.

b We use solar panels to recharge the ....

c The light was so bright that I had to .... my eyes.

d The information is .... electronically to the central computer.

e The labels can easily be .... from the package.

f The prices are .... for the two different phones.

3   Add the letters in the box to a–j to make words from Unit 20 in the Coursebook.

-al	-an	-ar	-ion	-ion	-less	-ness
	-rent		-text	-tion		

a   bill..........

b   con..........

c   cur..........

d   end..........

e   evolu..........

f   extern..........

g   nat..........

h   sol..........

i   urb..........

j   wit..........

4   Circle the most appropriate word from the two options in each sentence.

a   To understand this problem better, let's look at its *context / current*.

b   We used to have *external / endless* arguments about who was best at tennis.

c   This product was important in the *evolution / billion* of computer games.

d   Spacecraft are being sent to search for life in other *urban / solar* systems.

e   Anything plugged into a computer is called an *external / nation* device.

5   Use the **five** words you did *not* choose from Activity 4 in sentences of your own.

....

....

....

....

....

Language focus: Describing future events

Foundation

1   Draw lines to match the ways of describing future events with their functions.

A Use the *present simple* for	express a belief or an opinion.
B Use the *present continuous* for	a future plan or arrangement that's already decided.
C Use *will* to	plans and intentions.
D Also use *will* to	make an offer or a promise.
E Use *going to* for	predictions based on current evidence.
F Also use *going to* for	a future event that is scheduled or timetabled.

2   Match these sentences to the future forms in Activity 1.
Write the letter next to the sentence.

a   I'll call you later.   ☐

b   I'm going to take the bus to school.   ☐

c   I'm sure United will win the match.   ☐

d   It's definitely going to be a very hot day.   ☐

e   Our holidays start next week.   ☐

f   She's only having a small party for her birthday.   ☐

Practice

3 Make sentences by drawing lines to match the phrases.

Tomorrow morning I am playing	Don't worry, I'll clean it up.
Tomorrow I'm helping Dad in the garden so	I can just feel it.
After two months he's going to leave	I can't go with you.
Oh, sorry, the children have made a mess.	is going to be a problem.
Next week she's going to	plant some trees in her garden.
I think this crack on the wall	the country on a long trip.
This child will be someone important	when he grows up.
I know I'm going to be happy there,	basketball in the park.

4 Circle the most appropriate future form from the two options in these sentences.

a We *will have / have* an Italian lesson at 11 o'clock.

b We *will help / help* with the party preparations.

c When it is ready, this new technology *will provide / is providing* more energy.

d We *meet / are meeting* outside the park after school.

e I *am going to finish / am finishing* the exam before you. I'm sure of it!

f We *are receiving / will receive* our exam results in November.

g 'He's very busy right now.' 'That's okay, I *will wait / am waiting*.'

h My new course *starts / will start* on Monday at nine o'clock.

Challenge

5 Change the verbs in brackets into an appropriate future form. In some cases, there is more than one possible answer.

    a In August, the company .... (decide) what to do after the summer.

    b Listen! I think Christina .... (arrive).

    c There's so much to do. How are .... (finish) on time?

    d The movie .... (end) at 11 o'clock and then we can get a taxi home.

    e She .... (meet) her teacher during the second break.

    f So I .... (read) this and you do the planning, okay?

    g In the next 50 years, computers .... (continue) to change our lives.

    h I .... (clean) my bedroom when I get home from school.

6 Write **two** sentences for each of the six future forms in Activity 1.

....

....

....

....

....

....

....

....

....

....

Skills focus: Speaking

1 Skim the text 'Ten life-saving apps when living in Istanbul'. Match each app to these short descriptions.

a suggests local shopping locations ....

b finds the best routes on public transport...

c requests a taxi ....

d contains an online map ....

e uses a global positioning system ....

f helps find accommodation ....

g food deliveries ....

h suggests walking adventures ....

i tells you out about the city ....

j finds street art ....

Text 20.1

Ten life-saving apps when living in Istanbul

App 1: The must-have app for getting your favourite food delivered to your door. Whether you feel like durum, pizzas, lahmacun, kebab, tantuni, meze or sushi, a delivery person will jump on their scooter and slalom around the city's traffic to get your meal to you in 30 minutes or less. It has proven so popular that local people and expats would be panicking without it.

App 2: Traffic is probably the main cause of nervous breakdowns in the city and the reason we shouldn't blame taxi drivers for sometimes getting angry. Like a smart GPS helping you find the best routes through traffic, this app might be your best way to remain calm while finding your way through the crazy traffic!

App 3: This app uses your exact location to find the closest taxi and calls the driver with a single touch. It's practical, simple and offers payment choices such as cash or other credit sources. Another useful feature is a fare calculator, which can help ensure that the driver doesn't take you (and your wallet) for a ride.

App 4: This is a great app for those who like discovering the city in a spontaneous way without having to spend the whole stay with their nose stuck in a guidebook. All you need to do is to put on your headphones and enjoy the fascinating stories of lesser-known buildings of Istanbul. There's even an offline feature that allows you to use the app without an internet connection.

App 5: At first glance Istanbul might not seem to offer much to hikers, but the city is full of amazing places best seen on foot. This app includes a number of routes organised thematically, so you can visit all the city's main attractions without having to hop on a tour bus. If you are feeling extra adventurous, you can even create an original path and upload it for others to visit.

App 6: Trafi is a super-accurate app to find your way around the city with public transport. Tracking buses, trams, ferries and metro in real time and detecting traffic jams, it helps you to make the best choices when it comes to choosing a route and a method of transport to get from A to B.

App 7: Street art has become part of the city's visual landscape, with stunning murals on both sides of the Bosphorus. But these artworks are not always easy to find. The app has identified and listed locations in the city where you can spot the best graffiti with info on the local and sometimes international street artists behind them.

App 8: It's almost mission impossible to find your way in the impressive maze that is the Grand Bazaar and its shops. Worry no more. Filter your way through to find the kind of shop you're looking for, get info on the nearest ATMs and exchange office, save your favourite places to make your shopping experience at the Grand Bazaar much less overwhelming.

App 9: There are hundreds – if not thousands – of apps to find hotels, but this one is particularly effective because it is based in Turkey and is designed to find rooms at the last minute. So, if you urgently need a place to stay, this app could be just what you need.

App 10: While not exactly mind-blowing, this app could prove very useful when out and about in the city. It has the usual info about Istanbul's famous landmarks, the nearest shops, restaurants and hotels, and provides useful tips. The best thing about the app is that, unlike most other apps, your phone doesn't need to be connected to the internet to use it.

Adapted from www.timeoutistanbul.com

2 In which of the **ten** apps can you find the following pieces of information?

a Another useful feature is a fare calculator. ☐

b At first glance Istanbul may not seem to offer much to hikers. ☐

c Filter your way through to find the kind of shop you're looking for. ☐

d The app has identified and listed locations in the city where you can spot the best graffiti. ☐

e There are hundreds – if not thousands – of apps to find hotels. ☐

f This is a great app for those who like discovering the city in a spontaneous way. ☐

g Whether you're craving durum, pizzas, lahmacun, burgers, tantuni, meze or sushi . . . ☐

3 You are going to listen to Hakan and Gamze, two Turkish teenagers who live in Istanbul, talking about apps. As you listen, decide which of the apps you have read about would be most suitable for them. There are two apps for each speaker.

Gamze: ....

Hakan: ....

4   Choose **five** of the apps and think of a name for each one.

    ....

    ....

    ....

    ....

    ....

5   Have a discussion with a friend about which of the ten apps would be most useful for you.
    If this is not possible, try recording yourself making a short speech about the apps you
    think you would get the most use out of.

EXAM-STYLE QUESTION

Speaking, discussion

Look at the speaking card, which contains discussion questions on the topic of technology.

In pairs, decide who will play the interviewer and who will play the student. Then role play the interview.
The student playing the interviewer should ask the questions in the box. If you are doing this at home,
try recording your answers instead. Your discussion should last 3–4 minutes.

When you finish, change roles and role-play the discussion again.

> - Do you think that, in the future, everyone will have personal robots to help
>   around the house?
>
> - There is an opinion that using smartphone applications makes people lazy.
>   What is your opinion?
>
> - In many countries there is an age limit on when young people can have
>   their own social media account. Do you think this is a good idea?
>
> - In your opinion, does technology make learning easier?

〉Audioscripts

🎧 Unit 4 Skills focus

Speaker 1

Well, I've been driving my *boda-boda* for 15 years now and it has provided me and my family with a comfortable living. I'm a properly licensed driver and we get a lot of benefits. But in my town, Kampala, there are many drivers who are not licensed and they are a real danger both to themselves and everyone else. So many foreigners have accidents here, as they think it's great fun to rush around on a *boda-boda*, and many of them choose the cheapest driver, often with unfortunate consequences. It's just not worth it – pay a shilling or more extra and get a trained driver. And wear a helmet that fits properly! Despite this, I love my life as a *boda-boda* driver, as it's so free and I've got to know my city so well: the smells, the type of people in each area, the best roads . . . it's all in a day's work.

Speaker 2

I came to Uganda for work and had my first *boda-boda* experience from the airport where I was taken to my hotel along with my 25-kilogram suitcase on the back of my friend's *boda-boda*. Well, he became my friend after that nail-biting experience, as I kept throwing my arms around him because I was so frightened! We wove in and out of traffic, people, animals and other *boda-bodas*. On my bike, one passenger and a suitcase; on other bikes, four passengers! Huge bales of hay! One man sitting with a goat across his knee! Another, with a woman balancing two young children and a pair of chickens! Once I even saw a tiny new-born baby and its mother being taken from the hospital to their home – can you imagine what could have happened? I don't like to think about it.

Speaker 3

I had a couple of days in Kampala and the hotel recommended that I should ride with Dennis because he was the best person to help me get to know the city. He was brilliant and I had no idea that Kampala was such a vast and interesting place. Dennis took me to all the best parts and told me so much about the history and the people who live in Kampala; I couldn't have learnt more in a better way than I did in those three days. There were six of us in total travelling together, and we just let Dennis and his five colleagues decide what we would do, and what and where we would go each day. On day one we covered some of the main sights, including the Uganda Museum which told us all about the country's history from the Stone Age until today. We went to the Lubiri Palace on day two, an amazing place with plenty of history. On the third day we left the city to see the countryside, which was truly beautiful. Thank you, Dennis, you gave us a great time.

Speaker 4

I live and work in rural Uganda as a nurse and I'm like an ambulance on two wheels. We take people, especially pregnant women, from their homes to the local hospital. When I first started my job, what surprised me more than anything was how much trust people put in you – the patient and their family depend totally on you to get the sick person to the hospital on time. The pressure is constantly nagging me, because I know I'm driving quickly, but it's never *too* quickly. I'm careful to avoid all the potholes in the roads, the animals and children that keep running across your path, the deep puddles from the night's rainfall, and many other obstacles that can make the journey an extremely stressful one both for myself and for my passenger. But the feeling of elation when we arrive safely and I've delivered the patient to the doctors and nurses is amazing. I know that I've just done a good job.

🎧 Unit 4 Exam-style question

For my presentation, I'd like to talk about Raul Oaida, a young inventor from Romania. He was a fascinating person to investigate because he's very talented at teaching himself concepts that many engineers would find complex. And he's able to do this simply by accessing information that's on the internet. From an early age, he's been obsessed with going into space and would like to be an astronaut. This is the main reason he began inventing things.

Raul was only 14 when he decided to research how to build a jet engine. This is a type of engine for aircraft – it isn't suitable for cars as it uses too much fuel. Raul thought it would only take a few months to build, but it was three years before his design was fully functional. When he finally completed it, he fastened it to his bike and went for a ride!

At 16, Raul came up with another ambitious idea. He wanted to see if he could build a real spaceship. He figured out how to do this by reading lots of academic articles. And he was convinced that someone would finance his project. So the teen sent hundreds of messages on social networking sites to attract investors – many of them billionaires and CEOs.

A year later, an Australian businessman called Steve Sammartino became interested in Raul's spaceship project. When Steve learnt that the teenager was asking for $500 000, he politely refused and said to lower his expectations to less than $10 000. However, Raul revised his plan considerably and came back to Steve. This time he requested $1000 to put a toy spaceship into space. Steve agreed and sent Raul the money.

At 17, Raul proved to Steve that he was responsible enough to follow a strict budget and meet deadlines. Once Raul got all the materials he needed for the spaceship, he went to Germany to launch it into outer space. It also had a video camera to document the voyage. Raul posted a four-minute clip of the journey and got millions of views. This was the first time he attracted attention from the international news.

Soon, Raul was planning his next invention, while Steve was raising $40 000 so the teen could build a life-size car made out of Lego – small, plastic bricks that connect to create things. Importantly, air would be the only power source. Raul's invention would cost significantly more than the average price of a car. While this made it unrealistic for manufacturers to produce, Raul wanted to prove that anyone could invent a green vehicle.

After Raul finished building the car, it had to be flown to Australia. He was worried that while it was being transported, the engine might crack in half. Fortunately, that didn't happen. Although the car was made up of half a million plastic bricks, none of the parts got lost. It did come apart in many different places along the way, but once it arrived in Australia, Raul was able to put the car back together again.

Raul's unusual car made headlines around the world, showing that it's possible to build a 'green' vehicle out of toy bricks. But it won't win any races! Its maximum speed is 32 kilometres per hour, but the car is safer to drive at 28 kilometres per hour or lower. Raul's amazing Lego car works best at 27 kilometres per hour, which is slightly faster than the average cyclist!

🎧 Unit 5 Skills focus

Aphrodite: We're doing a speaking practice session next week and I'm a bit worried as I don't feel that I can prepare properly for it. Do you have any advice from when you did this at school last year?

Spiro: Let me think . . . Of course, worrying won't help! In fact, you can prepare a bit because the first part of the discussion is usually based on personal questions, which aren't there to challenge you.

Aphrodite: To be honest, I'm often really nervous if I feel I'm being judged on how well I'm speaking or if I'm making mistakes.

Spiro: Well, try to relax – no one is going to think badly of you if you don't get everything exactly right!

Aphrodite: But what if I'm asked something and I don't know how to reply in English? Can I say it in my own language?

Spiro: No, of course not! If you don't understand something, the best thing to do is to say so. Tell me what you would say if you don't understand.

Aphrodite: Hmmm . . . 'I'm sorry but I don't understand what you mean.'

Spiro: Excellent! Anything else?

Aphrodite: What about 'Could you repeat that please?' or 'Could you say that more slowly please?'

Spiro: Fantastic! It's much better to let the other person know you are having difficulties by using a correct English phrase than saying nothing at all.

Aphrodite: Thanks, that's good advice. But you know, I'm really worried that I just won't have enough to say.

Spiro: Well, it's important to keep speaking, but everyone gets nervous and whoever you're talking to will try and help you out.

Aphrodite: How?

Spiro: Well, the other person will probably have some questions ready to help you.

Aphrodite: What if I don't know anything about the topic they want to talk about?

Spiro: Actually, this practice isn't about your knowledge of the world; it's about your ability to communicate in English. So, if you're asked about a topic you feel uncomfortable with, such as global warming, then you could say, 'Actually, I don't feel I know very much about global warming but one thing I am aware of, which is connected, is the water problem in my country.'

Aphrodite: That's great, thank you. What about my pronunciation and my accent? I sound horrible! I feel I speak so differently to the people I hear on the news and on television.

Spiro: To be honest, nobody is asking you to have the perfect accent of a native speaker. The important thing is to speak clearly so that another person can understand you. I have no problem understanding you, so there's no need to worry!

Aphrodite: And what about my vocabulary? Do I know enough words?

Spiro: Actually, with both pronunciation and vocabulary it's always a good idea to speak and read as much as you can, both inside and outside the classroom.

Aphrodite: Thanks for all the advice!

Unit 5 Exam-style question

Recording 1
Recently, I went on a diving trip at the Great Barrier Reef. I didn't fully understand how much this industry is helping to protect the reef, but it's having a powerful effect, especially as commercial fishing isn't allowed in certain areas now. And as an experienced diver, I loved being able to concentrate on the incredible sea life instead of worrying about other things that might be going on around me. I saw many of the exotic fish that I hoped I would, too!

There are lots of things to consider when you book a diving tour on the Great Barrier Reef. It's better to go when there isn't heavy rain – the water's much clearer for diving then. It's cheaper during the wet season, but the experience won't be the same!

Recording 2
Mother: I hope you're looking forward to this food tour as much as I am!

Son: Actually, yeah – I can't wait!

Mother: Did I tell you that the tour goes to seven different locations for street food, which is good value considering what the other tours had to offer, although this one doesn't go to any restaurants that have won any awards. And it's just started up, so I didn't base my decision on the reviews.

Son: I'm sure it'll be fine. Besides, we both love doing this kind of thing when we're on holiday.

Mother: True – it's become a bit of a tradition and we've never been disappointed yet! I think it's a smart way to see somewhere new. The guides always know of these hidden secrets that are never in any guidebooks.

Son: That's exactly why I didn't have breakfast today – I'm ready to eat!

Recording 3
Interviewer: Ken Kalua teaches people how to surf volcanoes in Hawaii! So, is this actually a popular sport, Ken?

Ken: Yes, even though the average person wouldn't consider doing it! It tends to attract extreme athletes. They hear about it and have to try it, because it's not like anything else they've ever done – or are ever likely to do again! I think online posts of people surfing on lava actually put most people off, though.

Interviewer: For anyone brave enough, what advice can you give?

Ken: Well, it's essential to hire a thick body suit and surfboard, which are designed to protect you from severe heat. If you want to get the most out of surfing down lava, get as fit as possible – it'll help you control the surfboard better. There are hundreds of videos online; maybe check some out to see what's involved.

Recording 4
Good morning everyone! We're going to be leaving the hotel to visit Kruger National Park right after breakfast, so I need to give you some instructions. When we get to the park, you'll

see many incredible wild animals, including lions. It's important that you never get out of the van – under any circumstances. But don't worry about the heat, there's air conditioning to keep you comfortable and cold drinks and snacks are available.

We'll be heading to some excellent spots for taking photos, but please wait till we get there before opening the windows. When you do, don't try to attract the attention of the animals just for the sake of a good photograph. And if you want decent pictures, make sure that you switch off the clicking sounds on your cameras – wildlife can hear everything and may be scared away by such noises.

Recording 5

Girl: I heard you recently went to northern Canada.

Boy: Yeah, for a big dog-sled race that happens every year! Each competitor has 16 dogs to pull their sled – something people have been doing for thousands of years. I was dying to try it, so Dad asked a local guy to give me a lesson. It was exciting – especially learning the words that make the dogs turn left or right and go faster. That was unforgettable.

Girl: Cool! I'd love to go there someday. What's it like?

Boy: There was loads of snow, and Dad wasn't happy about driving in it for hours. Where we stayed was remote, but nice and cosy. This might sound odd, but I loved gazing at the stars in the freezing cold – they seemed so bright. It was strangely peaceful.

Unit 7 Skills focus

Speaker 1
I was living in France at the time because my parents and my two older sisters were working there, and so my interview for a place at a UK university had to be done online. I was absolutely terrified about the interviewers seeing me online, because I hate being photographed. I wonder how nervous I would have been if I'd been sitting in the same room as them! But I must have done okay because they offered me a place and I spent three very happy years studying there.

Speaker 2
I went for several university interviews and for most I was incredibly nervous. Five unsmiling faces waiting to interview me didn't help. For one interview, I had a pen in my hand which I kept chewing because of my nerves. Without knowing it, ink had leaked onto my face, and I didn't realise until afterwards when I saw myself in the mirror! I wish now that I'd taken a photograph. Not one of the interviewers said a word!

Speaker 3
My worst experience for a university interview was the wrong place, wrong date, wrong time. Unbelievable! To this day I still don't know how I managed to get everything so terribly wrong, even though I go over it in my head again and again and again. I guess perhaps I just had so much on my mind at the time that I got things mixed up. But I learnt a good lesson – never set off for an interview without checking and re-checking all the details!

Speaker 4
While I was having my university interview, one of the interviewers had a sneezing attack. At first, I managed to ignore it, but then I started to laugh and I didn't know how to stop myself. The situation only got worse as she continued sneezing every minute or so, and I felt incredibly rude for behaving like that. The other interviewer just continued the interview,

ignoring his colleague as if these sneezing fits were a common occurrence. He dealt with it far better than I did.

Speaker 5

My first interview for a university place is next week. I'm 100% prepared, and I've been online to check what I should and shouldn't do and say. I've also spoken to some of my teachers about how to approach the interview, and both my older sister and brother have already been through the same experience, so they also helped me get ready. I'm not sure what else I can do now, other than to be myself and try not to get too nervous, despite all my preparations.

Speaker 6

My worst university interview experience was one in which I was interviewed and filmed with seven others. We had to complete several tasks together. The idea, so they said, was to judge how we work with other people, but I felt it was very unfair. I'm not a very confident person so I hardly said anything, while the more confident people kept talking non-stop. The interviewers just let us get on with it for about 20 minutes. To my great surprise, they offered me a place!

Unit 7 Exam-style question

Interviewer: I'm talking to Sophie Watson, an academic coach who helps students to prepare for university interviews. Now, Sophie, what advice can you give about completing university application forms?

Sophie: This might sound like I'm stating the obvious, but everything on it must be correct – especially your grades, as universities will check these. Don't be afraid, however, to draw attention to your other achievements, such as volunteering and hobbies, and how you've benefited from them. On the other hand, don't fall into the trap of simply stating how passionate you are about a subject.

Interviewer: In general, is it quite common for universities to have interviews?

Sophie: That depends. Some universities have always held interviews as part of their selection process. Since the number of applicants increases each year, it wouldn't be realistic for all universities to interview every single person who applies. So, it tends to be particular degrees – such as medicine and primary education – that interview the most outstanding applicants to help decide who'll be offered a place.

Interviewer: I see. What should students do to prepare for a university interview?

Sophie: Definitely spend a lot of time and effort on getting ready for it – don't just show up! Of course, there are typical questions that you should be aware of, but don't write down your replies and learn them by heart or you won't sound natural on the day. The university will assume you have a certain level of knowledge, so read around the subject you want to study, as it shows you're taking an interest in where your subject goes, and this will get noticed.

Interviewer: Would you suggest that students practise doing interviews?

Sophie: Yes, I would. And ideally, you'd do this with someone who's been to a university interview before. They'll be able to offer you more informed advice than, say, your best mate. You want whoever's helping you to be honest about your performance, so you know which areas to work on. I think it's fair to say that everyone gets nervous at interviews, but you'll be even more anxious if you arrive completely unprepared.

Interviewer: Right. What's an interviewer actually assessing during the interview?

Sophie: Great question. Something to bear in mind is that their decisions aren't based on your manners, appearance or background. The interview is to see if you're able to think independently when they ask you questions. The interviewer wants to choose candidates who show potential in an area of study. It's not just about having the minimum requirements – the interviewer's looking beyond that.

Interviewer: I see. Now Sophie, is it a good idea to ask an interviewer questions?

Sophie: Absolutely. In fact, it's a wasted opportunity if you *don't* ask questions. However, it's important to avoid asking for information that you should already know, such as what's involved in the degree programme or what kind of assistance new students can expect. Go for something that shows the interviewer that you're up to date in a subject, and keen to know their opinion about a breakthrough in a recent study, for example.

Interviewer: So, is there anything students *shouldn't* do at the interview?

Sophie: Well, don't worry about pausing to think about a question before giving your reply. There's nothing wrong with this; in fact, it's desirable as it shows you're really considering what you want to say. And if your answer's quite long, the interviewer will let you know when it's time to move on. Make sure you let the interviewer steer the direction of the discussion, as that's their role.

Interviewer: And finally, once the interview is over, what should students do?

Sophie: While it's fresh in your mind, and before anything else, make some detailed notes about what you think you did well and how you could improve your performance for future interviews. This will also help when you compose a short letter to the university as a sign of courtesy for giving you the opportunity. There's no point in stressing about whether or not you'll be offered a place. Instead, be kind to yourself when going over everything that you did.

Interviewer: Thanks, Sophie. You've been extremely helpful.

🎧 Unit 10 Skills focus

When she got her exam results, Bimla knew that she wanted to go to university. But she had been worried that she would not be accepted by the other students once she got there. Although her teachers had always told her that she would do well at university, she nonetheless believed that other students would be better than her. 'I know I got good grades at school, but I thought that I would be left out by the other students,' she admits. Some of her friends thought she shouldn't even think about going to university, but she didn't agree with that and said: 'I think university should be for everyone, no matter where they come from or what their background is.'

Growing up in a large family, she'd always understood that her parents would depend on the children to contribute money to the home. 'We all knew we'd have to help pay the expenses at home, so when I told my parents I wanted to do my exams before going to university, they weren't very pleased initially,' she recalls. 'But they accepted the idea when they thought about the advantages of having a university graduate in the family.'

Money was short at home, so Bimla worked after her exams, saving nearly everything from her salary. She wanted to work in medicine, so she looked around and found a university nearby, which meant she could stay at home and study at the same time. It wasn't easy travelling to and from university each day, but she found that she could use the time sitting on the train in a constructive way. She had her favourite seat and would head straight for it when she got on the train. She would then know that she had a whole hour in which she could do some real studying, and since most people on the train were adults going to work, the atmosphere was usually peaceful. Between studying, travelling and going to work, she found that she had little time to socialise. But that wasn't a priority for her because she knew that she wasn't the only one making sacrifices for her studies, particularly when she saw her parents working all hours to help the family and knew that they were also doing this to support her as best they could.

The university had a good academic reputation and she thought she wouldn't get in, so she was very excited when she was offered a place. 'I never thought it possible,' she admits.

Three years later and she remembers her fears of being left out. 'I've made some really great friends, and everybody has been so helpful, even the lecturers! The idea that you are not good enough because you are different is so wrong – university is not like that.'

She wants to say to other families: 'If your child is good enough and really wants to go on to university, then you can't imagine the advantages there will be for you and your family.'

🎧 Unit 14 Skills focus

A modern matron: My cousin's enthusiasm for nursing convinced me to leave banking and start a nursing diploma. My first placement in elderly care was fascinating: the patients were as interested in me as I was in them. Delivering babies was particularly exciting, as I knew nothing about childbirth! Before I finished my diploma I was already planning my career.

I wanted a challenging focus where I'd really get to know my patients. Mental health seemed perfect: the patients love to talk, and the nurses don't wear uniforms. I like people knowing who I am simply by the way I handle myself.

To gain the right skills, I studied part-time for my nursing degree and then took a Master's in Transcultural Psychiatry. This special science gave me an idea of how mental illnesses and their treatment can be influenced by cultural and other factors.

I also spent a year as a unit manager in a private hospital, which really opened my eyes to financial management.

Two years later, these skills helped bring me to my current position as modern matron for a mental-health unit. People lose so much when they suffer from mental illness: jobs, relationships, physical health, even the ability to look after themselves. It's incredibly satisfying to help someone get their life back, watch them regain their skills and give them hope again.

Friends of mine in accounting and banking say they've never changed someone's life for the better. I have. On Sundays, they hate the idea of going to work the next day. I can't wait.

A community nurse: My second child had just been born when I discovered that a nursing course was starting nearby. Having worked in nursing homes and been frustrated by the limited level of care I could give, this seemed too good to pass up.

I began the course shortly after my baby was born and then took the chance to gain a career for life.

My first year as a qualified nurse was on a busy cancer ward, caring for very ill patients. I quickly learnt to manage my workload to stay focused on patient care, and to think on my feet. It was very challenging meeting new patients, managing chemotherapy and handling all the physical, social and emotional issues that accompany it. Incredibly rewarding too, but you have to be extremely organised to coordinate the high volume of testing, treatment and care that cancer patients need.

After such a challenging environment, I spent the next year in an orthopaedic outpatients unit with high numbers of less seriously ill patients. It was a good chance to experience a very different style of nursing in a different setting.

Now I'm doing something completely different again, as a support community nurse. Each morning I go to a particular location somewhere in my area and pick up the cases I'm to deal with that day. In a typical morning I'll visit up to eight patients in their own home, a clinic or a nursing home. No two days are alike.

Community nursing is a world away from hospital nursing. Observing and listening to patients in their own environment can help you pick up on other relevant issues. Every day, your knowledge, teaching and influencing skills are tested as you educate patients about the consequences of their choices. To anyone considering nursing as a career, I'd say try it: get some experience so you are realistic about what to expect.

Adapted from nursing.nhscareers.nhs.uk

Unit 14 Exam-style question

Recording 1
Mother: Congratulations on becoming a nurse. I'm so proud of you!

Son: Thanks, Mum! The degree was loads of hard work, but totally worth it. And I feel prepared from all the work experience I did at the hospital.

Mother: I didn't like that you went straight to lectures after such long shifts.

Son: I know. But that's how I learnt some essential skills – like how to make patients feel at ease and assisting doctors. I won't miss sitting in my room reviewing theory for hours on end, though. I found that particularly frustrating.

Recording 2
Father: Are you okay? You don't look very well?

Daughter: Oh . . . I feel terrible, Dad. I took an aspirin earlier when I was out for coffee with some friends. I guess it didn't work because my headache's getting worse.

Father: Then take it easy. Why don't you go and watch TV on the sofa for a while?

Daughter: Good idea, but I hope it won't be too bright. I should have known something wasn't right when the sun was bothering me on my way to meet everyone. Maybe I should have a short sleep.

Recording 3
Interviewer: Jake Jones is today's guest. He's competing in the Paralympic Games. Jake, have you always been into sport?

Guest: Absolutely! When I first learnt that I wouldn't regain the ability to walk after a skiing accident, I thought I'd never ski or do things like play tennis again. But I've found ways to do sports as a wheelchair user. You see, I started going to the track to build my upper-body strength because I wanted to be a stronger volleyball player, and now I'm doing this at an international level.

Recording 4
Professor: So, what area of medicine would you like to specialise in?

Student: Well, Professor, I've been doing lots of research to figure that out. At first, I was convinced that I wanted to do paediatric medicine, because I love working with children. Then I got to see how incredible it is to help people with physical disabilities to have a better quality of life. I'm keen to do that. After a lot of thought, I'm certain that performing surgery or spending my career in a lab wouldn't be as rewarding.

Recording 5
Doctor: What's the problem?

Patient: I hurt my leg when I was running, Dr Stewart.

Doctor: Right, I'll put pressure on different areas of your leg. Tell me where you feel pain. I'll start with the knee. How's that?

Patient: It hurts but it's not too bad.

Doctor: How about the ankle?

Patient: That's extremely painful.

Doctor: Does it feel the same in the heel?

Patient: Umm . . . Almost as much.

Doctor: Now move your toes for me. How does that feel?

Patient: It's nearly as bad as my heel. It really aches!

Doctor: I see. I think we need to take some X-rays.

Recording 6
Reporter: When Alanna Turner first arrived at her new school, she realised that it didn't have any electric doors. These make getting in and out of school for wheelchair users much easier. Now Alanna's raised over $8000 to have them installed. Most teens might sell T-shirts or ask for donations. Instead, she organised an event where students paid a fee to rent a wheelchair for the day to get to their classes. This, of course, was a huge success, which is why the evening news is doing this special report on Alanna.

Recording 7
Female: Are you coming to the team meeting?

Male: Yeah – just finishing some paperwork.

Female: That's my least favourite job as a paramedic. A busy shift means that there are more forms to fill in for every patient that we see.

Male: I'm actually writing a formal complaint to take to the meeting.

Female: Why's that?

Male: Half the things, including basic stuff like bandages and medicine, weren't in the ambulance at the start of my shift.

Female: That's happened to me recently! I'll bring this up too – someone's failing to do a pretty essential job.

Male: Yeah, it's shocking!

Recording 8

Male: Hey Sara. You look exhausted. Why don't you take a break?

Female: I've got other things to do that are a bit more urgent than sleeping!

Male: Like what? I'm on my way to see Dr Patel to discuss a patient's X-ray.

Female: I've just been in to see him, actually. He wants me to look up a rare heart condition in the medical library, which I'll do, but I wish I wasn't absolutely starving!

Male: I know – let's have lunch in the canteen after we get these jobs out of the way.

Female: All right.

🎧 Unit 19 Skills focus

Last week, our fashion and style reporter, Tammy Smith, spent some time with Giovanni Conte, who was last year voted the most influential designer of the millennium (so far!). Here's what happened when they met up at the Royal Hotel.

Tammy Smith: Giovanni, is it true that the clothes industry is stuck in the past?

Giovanni Conte: Most definitely! For example, although the actual fibres we use in producing materials have changed considerably over the centuries, the clothes-making process itself is basically the same: spin the fibre into thread, weave the thread into cloth, cut it into pieces and then sew it back together again to make an item of clothing. Very simple, really.

Tammy: But I understand that all this is about to change, isn't it?

Giovanni: That's my plan, yes, and it's incredibly exciting. I've got together with GHK Electrics and the Jeane Company to produce a range of technical clothing. We've included GHK mobile-phone and MP3 technology in a range of jackets designed by me and made by the Jeane Company.

Tammy: But mobile-phone and MP3 technology in clothes? How does that work?

Giovanni: Well, the jackets, which will soon be available in shops all over the world, will feature phones that can be dialled using voice-recognition technology, and a microphone and earphones built into the hood or collar. The MP3 player automatically stops when the phone rings, like on an aircraft when an announcement is made. Everything is controlled via a keypad hidden beneath a pocket flap.

Tammy: But what happens when the jacket gets dirty?

Giovanni: The whole range is totally machine-washable and very fast-drying.

Tammy: Where do you get your design ideas from?

Giovanni: Over the years, I've collected clothes from all over the world and, in my studio in Bologna, I have a wardrobe of more than 50 000 garments, mostly military uniforms, which provide me with inspiration for my designs.

Tammy: Apart from the phone and MP3 player, what else could be included in your designs?

Giovanni: Currently, I'm looking into the possibility of building in a face-recognition camera, which would provide you with information about a person when you meet them again.

Parents could keep an eye on their children through tiny cameras. And all this technology would be invisible. It won't be long before all clothes contain some sort of micro-computer.

Tammy: But with all this in-built technology, will clothes still look fashionable?

Giovanni: Of course! It's very important that clothes look beautiful, so I have tried to achieve the right balance between fashion and usefulness.

🎧 Unit 19 Exam-style question

Speaker 1
I'm glad that more people are becoming aware of the negative impacts of fast fashion. Now that I know more about them, I try whenever possible to buy from brands that are helping to save the planet. However, one of the ways that I express myself is through my clothes, and that's really important to me, so it's annoying that I'm not allowed to do that during term time. I wish we didn't have to follow such strict regulations – I hate wearing the same thing as everyone else.

Speaker 2
My girlfriend's really into fashion and she always looks amazing. But she isn't impressed by my fashion sense, and hints at this by buying me fashion magazines. My friends and I skateboard everywhere, so we're always in T-shirts, joggers and trainers – that's *our* uniform. Sure, we're probably covered head to toe in skater brands, but they design clothes especially for skaters that actually look cool. Maybe one day I'll try to find my own style, but I really can't see that happening any time soon.

Speaker 3
It's crazy how quickly trends change, and I was obsessed with keeping up with them. It's kind of embarrassing to admit, but I was spending way too much energy on trying to copy whatever my favourite celebrities wore. Then I quit social media to see what life would be like without it – and I've never looked back! And actually, I quickly realised that I shouldn't be caring about this stuff, as it's so trivial. There are far more serious things to be concerned about than what I'm wearing – like global warming, for example!

Speaker 4
To be honest, I don't mind that I wear a school uniform. It means that I have less to think about when I'm getting ready in the morning. You wouldn't know this because I'm really into fashion and want to study it at college. Sewing stuff started as a fun thing to do with my granny, but it grew into more than a hobby. In fact, I've made nearly all the clothes I own. One day, I hope to have my own brand that celebrities want to wear.

Speaker 5
I don't know anyone around my age who doesn't care about the way they look, and fashion plays a big part in that. I wish I didn't buy into fast fashion, but there's no way I can afford the brands that models wear in fashion magazines. When I've saved up enough to buy new clothes, I only go for the trendiest labels because that's what my mates wear. Maybe I care a bit too much about their opinions. That's probably why I like wearing my school uniform so much.

Speaker 6
I'm glad to see that more and more fashion magazines are featuring eco-friendly brands. They help to show me and my friends that there are better options out there. Not long ago, I was only willing to buy the latest styles, because I thought this was more important. Then I started looking at posts by stars like Emma Watson and Rosario Dawson, who wear clothes that aren't

damaging the environment. I'm not only inspired by what they wear, I'm also trying to be more conscious when I buy new clothes.

🎧 Unit 20 Skills focus

Gamze: I need something to help me get around town quickly and without having to wait too long for public transport, and I want to be able to pay online. Also I want to know in advance how much I'm going to have to pay, if possible. Do you think there's an app to do that for me?

Hakan: Yes, I'm sure you'll find something suitable. I'm more interested in sightseeing. Even though I was born here in Istanbul and I've lived here all my life, I really don't think I know very much about its history and what it has to offer. I want an app that will show me all of Istanbul's hidden places, and if I can avoid having to stare at my phone screen, that would be great.

Gamze: What else? I'd like an app for shopping – something that will guide me through Istanbul's biggest market. Even though I live in Istanbul, I usually get lost inside the market.

Hakan: Me too! It's impossible! My other must-have app is for finding my way around the city itself. Every week there seems to be a new road layout, and the city is changing so rapidly that sometimes I don't recognise places any more. Obviously I don't drive yet but I love walking, so an app that shows me all the best places, and without having to be online, would be really useful.

> Acknowledgements

We would like to thank the following authors for their contributions: Tom Bradbury for writing the reading and writing exam-style questions; Katia Carter and Tim Carter for writing the speaking exam-style questions; Jude Alden for writing the listening exam-style questions.

We would like to thank the following reviewers for providing feedback on the draft manuscript: Audrey Cowan, Anna Davies, Wenlian Yang and Aga Gurbin.

The authors and publishers acknowledge the following sources of copyright material and are grateful for the permissions granted. While every effort has been made, it has not always been possible to identify the sources of all the material used, or to trace all copyright holders. If any omissions are brought to our notice, we will be happy to include the appropriate acknowledgements on reprinting.

Test 6.1 adapted from 'Why teenagers can't get up in the morning' by Fiona MacRae, published on 30/08/2006. Used with the permission of dmg media licensing; **Text 13.1** adapted from 'Felix Baumgartner: watch the jump', October 2012, ©Telegraph Media Group Limited 2012. Used with permission; **Unit 14 Skills focus** audio content adapted from nursing.nhscareers.nhs.uk (contains public sector information licensed under the Open Government License v3.0); **Test 15.1** Adapted from content © The Nemours Foundation/KidsHealth. Reprinted with permission; **Text 20.1** adapted from p. 48 of *Time Out Istanbul*, May 2015, reprinted by permission of Time Out England Limited.

Thanks to the following for permission to reproduce images:

Cover Andriy Onufriyenko/GI; *Inside* **Unit 1:** AlexLMX/GI; JohnnyGreig/GI; Richard Drury/GI; **Unit 2:** Adventtr/GI; Mohamad Adning's/GI; **Unit 3:** Vgajic/GI; Etiennevoss/GI; **Unit 4:** Westend61/GI; **Unit 5:** Claudia Feudi/GI; Brian Cockley/GI; **Unit 6:** GCShutter/GI; **Unit 7:** Dirk Hoffmann/GI; Skynesher/GI; **Unit 8:** Martin-dm/GI; GCShutter/GI; **Unit 9:** B.S.P.I./GI; **Unit 10:** Peter Dazeley/GI; PeopleImages/GI; **Unit 11:** Sachin Polassery/GI; Hulton Deutsch/GI; **Unit 12:** Peter Adams/GI; Image Source/GI; **Unit 13:** PK-Photos/GI; Carlosgaw/GI; Kevin Winter/GI; **Unit 14:** Peter Dazeley/GI; **Unit 15:** 2A Images/GI; **Unit 16:** Life On White/GI; Yuji Sakai/GI; **Unit 17:** Tajinder Singh Thiara/GI; Monty Rakusen/GI; **Unit 18:** Kittiphan Teerawattanakul/GI; **Unit 19:** Cdwheatley/GI; **Unit 20:** Luis Alvarez/GI

GI = Getty Images